LANCASTER CANAL WALKS

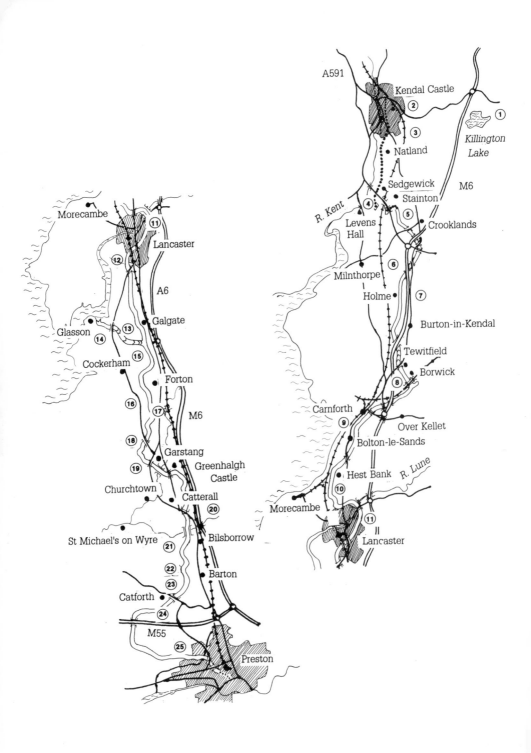

LANCASTER CANAL WALKS

by

MARY WELSH

Illustrations by

CHRISTINE ISHERWOOD

CICERONE PRESS
MILNTHORPE, CUMBRIA

© Mary Welsh 1993
ISBN 1 85284 138 9
A catalogue record for this book is available from the British Library.

Front Cover: ' ... the magnificent Lune Aqueduct ... carries the canal
51ft above the River Lune'

PREFACE

It is always a joy to walk the Lancaster Canal towpath. For much of its route the waterway cuts through glorious countryside. Passing through hamlets, villages, towns and a city, it was constructed in the late eighteenth century as a link between industrial centres so that heavy, bulky commodities could be delivered speedily. In 1833 horse-drawn packet boats carried passengers the 57 miles from Preston to Kendal in seven hours.

The canal passes through Cumbria and Lancashire, using the most convenient route with no thought for walkers, naturalists and ornithologists who, 200 years on, come to enjoy this long-distance way.

The walks in this book are circular. Part of each walk is along the towpath - every foot of which is covered - but each takes the walker also into the lovely Lancashire or Cumbrian countryside. I have walked beside the cut in every season and described the bird and plant life to be seen throughout the year. In each walk I have described the canal in a specific month.

None of the walks is arduous but a few climb gentle limestone slopes. At some times of the year the cart-tracks can be very muddy. Good footwear is always advisable.

My thanks go to Tom, my husband, and to Maureen Fleming and Joan Morgan, two good friends who have accompanied me on my researches.

My thanks go also to Christine Isherwood, whose drawings have so faithfully and delightfully captured the very essence of the walks along the cut.

White water lilies (Walk 1)

Meadow cranesbill and hayrattle (Walk 1)

CONTENTS

Key to maps 8

M/S Scales 9

7½   1.   Around Killington Lake 11

2½   2.   Canal Head to K Shoe factory via Kendal Castle .. 15

6½   3.   Hincaster to K Shoe factory, Kendal 19

4   4.   Stainton to Levens Park .... 24 ✓

5   5.   Stainton to Endmoor 28

i0   6.   Crooklands to Holme 32

i0-11   7.   Holme to Saltermire Bridge via Hutton Roof 38

10-11   8.   Tewitfield to Carnforth 43

6½   9.   Carnforth to Hest Bank 49

5½   10.   Hest Bank to the Lune Aqueduct 53

8   11.   Lune Aqueduct to Aldcliffe 57

7   12.   Galgate to Aldcliffe 62

4½   13.   Conder Green picnic site to Galgate .... 66 ✓

4½   14.   Conder Green via Glasson Dock .... 69 ✓✓

5   15.   Cockerham to Thurnham .... 73 ✓✓

7½   16.   Cockerham to Forton 77

5½   17.   Forton to Scorton 81

7   18.   Ford Green to Cabus Nook 85

8½   19.   Garstang to Ford Green and Catterall 89

7½   20.   Catterall via Claughton-on-Brock 94

5   21.   Around Brock .... 98 ✓

4½   22.   Carefoot to Hollowforth .... 102 ✓

3½   23.   Swillbrook to Woodplumpton .... 106 ✓

7   24.   Swillbrook to Salwick 110

8   25.   Circular Walk from Preston 115

Key to maps

- - → - -	Arrows indicate direction of walk
	Canal (+ bridge)
	Motorway (or dual carriageway)
	Road
	Railway (+ station)
	River
	Tracks
- - - - -	Footpath
	Building
	Built-up area
	Deciduous wood
	Coniferous wood
	Parkland
	Limestone pavement
	Lake (or estuary)
	Saltmarsh
	Significant cliff (usually a quarry)
	Mound (usually with ruin)

Scales

All maps are at a scale of 1 : 50,000
except number 2 (Kendal) which is at 1 : 25,000

Anxious sandpiper and house martins

Killington Lake

1: Around Killington Lake

Distance:	7¹/₂ miles
Time:	4-5 hours
Parking:	Lay-by on A684, east of M6
Terrain:	Easy walking but some pasture can be very wet
Map:	Pathfinder SD 617 69/79 Sedburgh & Bough Fell
	Outdoor Leisure 7 The English Lakes S.E.

K illington Lake, a reservoir that covers more than 150 acres, was constructed to supply water to the Kendal end of the canal. It was completed in 1819 and holds 761 million gallons. Its water enters the Peasey Beck and reaches the canal at Crooklands. The canal is carried over the Peasey by the Crooklands Aqueduct, and the feeder comes in just beyond it.

Leave Kendal by the A684. Cross the M6 and park in the large well signposted lay-by on the left. Walk to the bottom of the hill and pass through a gate on the left. Walk the rough track, a bridleway, which

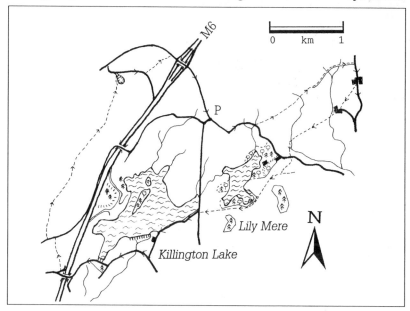

Lily Mere

Killington Lake

Curlews

soon becomes a pleasing grassy way with a spectacular view of the Howgills. Tormentil spangles the pastures and curlews and green plovers fly overhead, calling to their mates incubating eggs.

Beyond the fourth gate the track becomes wet and you will need to step from one tuft to the next. After 50 yards the cart-track is reinforced and the way is a pleasure to walk once more. Continue past a small fir plantation, cross the narrow Capplethwaite Beck and continue to a gate onto a moorland road.

Turn right to walk downhill, with a pleasing view of the Lune valley ahead. Pass the farmhouse at New Field and take the waymarked gate on the right, beyond the farm buildings. Walk ahead, keeping beside the wall on the right. Climb the stile in the boundary wall into a glorious hay-meadow where grow cranesbill, buttercup, cow parsley and many flowering grasses. Keep left to follow the wall round to a gate. Beyond stride ahead to a barn which you walk around right, to join the access road to Ghyll Farm.

Walk the road right to pass to the right of the farm. Cross a small footbridge over the Capplethwaite, which tumbles noisily through its tree-lined gill. Pass through the gate beyond and walk the farm track to the next gate. Beyond, strike diagonally right to cross rough pasture to reach a small ford over the Priestfield Beck just at the junction of two walls. Cross the narrow stream and turn left. Continue ahead where lousewort flowers, keeping parallel with the deepening gill, bright with blossoms of hawthorn and rowan.

Aim for the broken stile to the road in the wall ahead, following the indistinct path. Cross the A684 with care to a gate. Beyond, follow the cart-track, signposted Killington Lake, up the slope to a gate, from where there is a good first view of Lily Mere and the lake. Notice the interesting footpath signs fixed to the fence at varying intervals. Pass through the gate and look right for delightful glimpses of Lily Mere through mixed woodland.

Where the track swings left over the moor, continue ahead. Cross a small ford and walk on over a very wet area where there is no sign of a path, then over a small footbridge. Beyond, a wide, clear grassy way continues ahead close to the plantation that clothes the southern end of the mere where water lilies grow. From the trees come the calls of willow warblers, tree pipits and a cuckoo. Continue past another footpath sign and follow the track, which gradually drops downhill, through another wet area, to Old Scotch Road.

Cross, and continue ahead along a lane, which is lined with summer flowers and runs beside Killington Lake. Continue past the sailing centre and then the dam on the right. Follow the lane as it swings right to pass the outlet from the dam where water joins the Peasey Beck and crowfoot flowers in profusion. Climb the lane past water avens growing in the verge and turn right at the T-junction. Walk on to pass another dam on the right. At the next T-junction turn right to cross the road bridge over the M6.

Stride ahead past a small plantation and take the gate to a farm track on the right. Walk ahead and pass through a gate on the left, set in a wall. Climb straight uphill over a huge pasture, away from the noise of the M6, to a gate to the fell road. Enjoy the splendid view from here of Killington Lake in its entirety.

Turn left and walk 50 yards to the signposted bridleway on the right. Walk the wide track beyond to a gate and continue ahead to a gate in the right corner of the next pasture. Beyond strike ahead with the wall to your right.

Pass through the next gate and stroll on, keeping a new fence to your left. On reaching a wall ahead, walk right beside it to a gate, which you pass through to a wide cart-track. Follow this as it descends to a new gate to the right. Beyond, turn right to walk downhill on the old road to pass through a gate on the left. Walk ahead, keeping to the left of a narrow stream which you cross towards the field edge. Walk right to a gate to the A684. Turn right to cross the M6. Continue ahead, where hay rattle flowers in the grass verge, to rejoin your car.

Kendal Castle

2: Canal Head to K Shoe Factory via Kendal Castle

Distance:	2¹/₂ miles
Time:	1¹/₂ hours
Parking:	New Road Kendal, close to the River Kent
Terrain:	Easy walking most of the way. Steep climb to the castle.
Map:	Landranger 97 Kendal to Morecambe

Continue south from New Road along the A65. Cross the bridge over the lovely river and continue along Aynam Road. Turn left into Queen Katharine Street and walk towards the castle to reach the site of the Lancaster to Preston Canal.

The canal, designed by John Rennie, was opened in 1819 and was in use until 1938. Sadly this stretch of the canal was filled in in 1955, but the route has been preserved by constructing a cycle way along the cut. Several bridges are all that remain in this area to remind us of the once grand waterway.

Walk north from the car park, along a good track, to Canal Head, now the site of a civic amenity centre where you can play tennis, view the intrepid on the dry-ski slope - or tip your rubbish. The name seems at first to be the only evidence that the canal existed. But more concrete evidence is provided by the factories, dating from both last century and this, clustered together around the basin. They sprang up because coal could be carried by boats into the heart of the industrial area to power its diverse activities.

Return along the track. To the left, on their huge glacial mound, stand the ruins of Kendal Castle. Pass

Celandines

Indian
balsam

under the first of the canal bridges. Continue ahead along the cycle way, passing a factory on the right and a cemetery on the left. Cross and continue along the wide way. Ahead lies the second canal bridge, Kendal Change or Changeline Bridge. A cobbled way, on the right, swings out and up over the bridge, once enabling canal horses to pass to the towpath on the opposite bank. Such bridges are called turnover bridges.

The track leads out into more open country, with playing fields to the right. Look across, beyond the fields, to a mock Tudor house built in the style of the Netherfield Toll House. The houses of Heron Hill lie to the left of the track. Continue below a row of beeches to cross the A65. Head along the cycle track, which is lined with Indian balsam. In icy weather, water was released from this stretch of the canal to flood a field for skating. Now the housing estate built on the field is called the Rinkfield Estate.

Pass below the next bridge, which is festooned with dark-leaved ivy. Step out along the track. It passes beneath a row of magnificent beeches, with a large crop of inky cap fungi below. Here a signboard tells you that you are 14 miles from Tewitfield and 1 mile from Kendal. At the end of the track cross the Natland Road and walk on to where the footpath turns right through a hedge. This is the point where you leave the canal footpath in Walk 2.

Retrace your steps along the cycle way, enjoying the views over the town and away to Benson Knott. Cross Parkside Road and turn right to walk the path at the side of the road, beside a cemetery wall. Continue where it rises above the road and then drops again. Turn left to climb steps that lead to a quiet reinforced track running between two cemeteries. The track is lined with rhododendrons, holly and yew and in autumn a deep carpet of bronzed leaves rustles beneath your feet.

Walk to the kissing gate, which gives access to a path rising sharply to the edge of the moat surrounding the castle. Today the

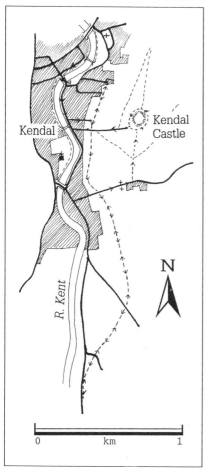

moat, which once was lined with spikes and other deadly objects, is grazed by friendly cows.

Bear left to walk the wide grassy track that edges the moat until you come to a gate by which you can enter the grassy area within the ruined wall. The original entrance was probably by a drawbridge and a portcullis. The castle was built by an early Baron of Kendal, possibly Gilbert Fitz Reinfreed, Sheriff of Lancaster, between 1205 and 1215. Katherine Parr, the surviving wife of Henry VIII, spent a very happy childhood there. The castle was acquired by the town and opened to the public to mark Queen Victoria's diamond jubilee in 1896.

Wander around the site and imagine the hurly-burly within the walls when the castle was in its heyday. Leave by the gate and turn left to walk a third of the way round the moat. Then take the stepped path that drops downhill to another kissing gate. Beyond, walk down Sunnyside. Look for stone steps on the left side of the canal bridge. Turn right to pass under the bridge and then left into Queen Katherine Street to regain your car.

Ink cap fungi

17

River Kent

3: Near Hincaster to K Shoe Factory, Kendal

Distance:	6¹/₂ miles
Time:	3¹/₂ hours
Parking:	Lay-by by gate to Levens Park on road to Hincaster
Terrain:	Easy walking all the way. Riverside path could be muddy.
Map:	Pathfinder 627 SD 48/58 Milnthorpe Outdoor Leisure 7 The English Lakes S.E.

This walk first follows the route of the Lancaster Canal for 3¹/₂ miles through flower-filled meadows, then takes you back beside the wide, chuckling, gracefully curving River Kent.

The canal, a magnificent feat of engineering, was built in the eighteenth century. Once horse-drawn barges hauled coal, lime (giving it the nickname, the black and white canal), slate or timber along the canal to Preston, Lancaster or Kendal. The "cut", narrow, straight and bridged, contains no water - alas. In some places the "cut" has disappeared.

To park, leave Kendal by-pass at the Sedgwick round-about, taking the exit for Sedgwick. In ¹/₄ of a mile take the right turn, signposted Hincaster, cross above the by-pass and park on the right in a

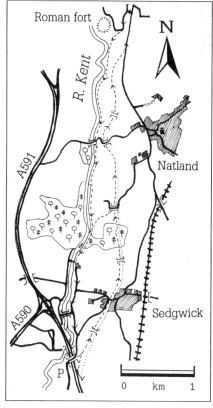

'Stranded' bridge

lay-by close to an entrance to Levens Park. Walk back across the bridge to a stile on the right at the top of a small bank. The footpath is signposted Hawes Bridge.

Once over the stile - a rather high one - strike uphill, bearing slightly to the right. At the fence, turn left and walk ahead towards a canal bridge seemingly "stranded" in a sea of grass. Sedgwick House (built by the Wakefield family, who owned the Wakefield Gunpowder Works at Sedgwick, in 1868) lies to the left. Pass through the kissing gate below the bridge and there is the canal with its towpath and its cut, now supporting a glorious display of reeds, forget-me-nots and yellow iris. Both are hedged with willows, hawthorn, elder, rose, oak and hazel, which resound with birdsong.

The towpath continues above Sedgwick, with its warm stone houses and cottage gardens. Here, on the busy canal, horses were changed and stabled in the village. Lean on the aqueduct and look at the sturdy steps that lead down to the village. After passing more houses, where the cut is used as a builder's yard and as garden extensions, climb a stile into a hay meadow. Here, confusingly, there is no trace of the canal. Only a forlorn Horse Park Bridge remains, surrounded by rolling pastures where curlews call and fly overhead.

Walk onto a stile into deciduous woodland of Larkrigg Spring and stride along the grassy path above the outline of the canal. Beyond the wood the towpath continues, to pass beneath Larkrigg Hall Bridge, bordered with pink clover, dog daisies, and blue and mauve cranesbill. The stiled path continues to Natland. Pass under Crowpark Bridge and follow the signpost directions for Kendal.

From now on the canal outline can be seen intermittently. In the dense hedge on the left of the towpath whitethroats sing quietly and a great tit parent feeds several youngsters. Pass beneath Natland Hall Bridge.

At the finish of the path, at Natland Road, walk ahead to the end of the K Shoe factory and follow the footpath sign, pointing left, for Hawes Bridge. (Before you leave the road notice that the outline of the canal can still be seen below the beech trees on the opposite side and look for a canal bridge tall among the houses.)

The footpath passes beside the factory to the River Kent, where there is a first sighting of giant hogweed. Turn left and walk along the back of the buildings. Follow the yellow waymarks to a lane. Turn right and walk down to a footpath sign pointing left across a meadow to a squeeze stile. Beyond, a high level path continues below trees, with the Kent flowing cheerily below. Here young house martins scream deliriously as they feast on a myriad of insects and a sandpiper calls warningly to its brood.

River Kent

The easy-to-follow path, edged with a host of summer flowers, keeps beside the river to a lane leading to Natland. Turn right and walk the few yards to stand on Hawes Bridge. Look down to the white-topped falls below and then return to the footpath, signposted Force Bridge, to continue downstream.

The path soon rises high above the river that lies hidden at the bottom of wooded slopes. These fail to deaden the noise of the Kent descending the slopes in spectacular rapids. Stride on where the path passes through open fields and the hedgerow supports water avens and comfrey. Pass through the gap stile to a wide cart track and walk ahead. Below, the river swirls around a small island crowded with giant hogweed. Walk on past an elegant footbridge, to the narrow lane that leads to Sedgwick Road.

Walk ahead, continuing along the road to Hincaster. Cross the bridge over the by-pass to return to your car.

Irises and water avens

Oak avenue, Levens Park

4: From Stainton via Levens Park

Distance:	4 miles
Time:	2-3 hours
Parking:	Lay-by at water's end Stainton
Terrain:	Easy walking all the way. Could be muddy after rain.
Map:	Pathfinder 627 SD 48/58 Milnthorpe

This walk explores more of the once busy waterway where the dark, placid water has long gone (drained in 1955), and has been replaced by lush vegetation supporting a myriad of wild life.

Leave the Kendal by-pass at the Sedgwick roundabout. Drive through the village of Sedgwick, pass under the aqueduct and take the second right turn to pass under the railway bridge. Turn right at the next crossroads, at Crosscrake. Just before the bridge over the canal, turn left and park on the right in a large, slightly reinforced area. Here you obtain your only glimpse, on this walk, of the canal with water.

Walk round the end of the water to the far side. Pass through the gate under the bridge (Stainton Crossing) and continue along the raised, grassy towpath in the direction of Kendal (west). In spring the grass below the hawthorn hedge is spangled with celandines and in

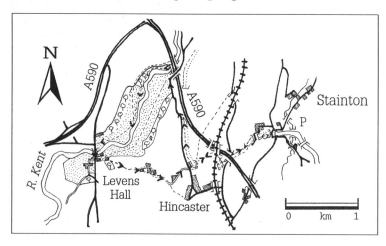

Hincaster Tunnel

late autumn the trees are heavy with berries.

Climb the slightly awkward stile below Sellet Hall Bridge and continue to a stile onto the narrow Wells Head Lane that passes below the A590. Turn left and walk under the bridge and then take the signposted footpath on the right that passes through larch woodland. Ahead lies the opening to the Hincaster Tunnel.

The tunnel, designed by John Fletcher and built by William Crossley, was constructed to serve the needs of the Wakefield Gunpowder Works at Sedgwick. The 378-yard-long tunnel, completed in 1817, was driven through Tunnel Hill, a huge drumlin. It required 4,000,000 bricks for its vaulted roof and these were made on the site from clay dug at Moss Farm, a mile away. The parts of the tunnel under water, were lined with limestone.

Climb the viewing platform to obtain a good view through the tunnel. Continue along the path which leads uphill and to the left of the tunnel. It first passes beneath a small bridge and then continues through a long passageway below the railway line. This would have been the route taken by the horses, the tunnel having no towpath. The boats were pulled through the tunnel by a chain fixed to the wall. Later this was replaced by a rope which was attached by rings fixed to the south wall.

At the top of the slope, climb the stile and cross a muddy farm track to the stile opposite. Continue along the grand path between the hedgerows as the horses did so long ago. In spring look for both purple and white violets growing close to moss-covered boulders.

Pass beneath a farm bridge (high enough to allow a horse to walk below) and then drop downhill almost to the road. Turn right and walk along a narrow path, behind dwellings, that leads to the towpath once more and the other end of the tunnel. Look for the illustrated interpretative panel on the huge portal of dressed stone, similar to that found at the other end.

Turn left and continue along the towpath, following it as it veers to the right. Look back for a good view through the tunnel. Here among reeds and bulrushes small songbirds flit. The long straight path continues through a wooded area, passing beneath some splendid sweet chestnut trees.

Leave the old towpath at the signpost and walk for $1/2$ a mile along the Hincaster to Sedgwick road - the A590 obliterating the canal for some distance. At the gates to Levens Park, on the left (where you parked for the previous walk), pass through the small gate and bear to the left to walk between an avenue of oaks. On either side black fallow deer graze with sheep. Look for the footpath sign that directs you nearer to the side of the River Kent, which is bordered by magnificent beech trees.

Continue to the small gate to the verge at the side of the A6. Turn left and walk a few yards to the footpath sign pointing the way to return to Hincaster. A wide reinforced farm track leads gently uphill to High Barns. Just before the attractive dwelling look for the stone stile through the wall on the right. Stride on keeping the farm buildings to the left, to pick up a good track that swings to the right across rolling pasture land. Look across left to Sedgwick House.

At a junction of tracks bear to the left to pass Hincaster Hall. The track continues downhill between hedgerows to the road. Cross over and take the horsepath, walked earlier, to the right, climbing uphill. From here retrace your outward route to Stainton and another tantalising glimpse of the canal with water.

'Black fallow deer graze ...'

Larches by Canal

5: Stainton to Endmoor

Distance:	5 miles
Time:	2¹/₂ hours
Parking:	Lay-by at water's end at Stainton
Terrain:	Easy walking for all the way. Short climb out of Endmoor.
Map:	Pathfinder 627 SD 48/58 Milnthorpe

The last three walks along the route of the once busy Lancaster Canal passed through Kendal and through pleasing countryside beside the waterless cut. This walk starts where the water starts.

Leave the Kendal by-pass at the Sedgwick roundabout and continue to the village. Drive under the aqueduct and take the second right turn to pass beneath the railway bridge and then turn right again, at Crosscrake. Continue down the lane, passing the school on the right. Just before the bridge over the canal, turn left and park on the right in a large, slightly reinforced area beside the canal, here water-filled, at Stainton.

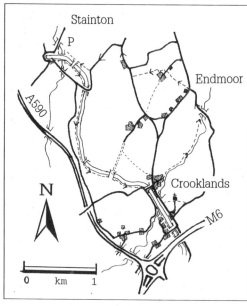

Walk round the end of the canal to the far side, where a signpost says 6 miles to Kendal and 9 to Tewitfield. Stride along the wide grassy path, where gorse is laden with blossom and hazel catkins and pussy-willow bloom. Look for St Sunday's Beck racing below the aqueduct on its way to add to the waters of Peasey Beck.

This glorious, easy-to-walk path continues on and on, passing under Stainton Bridge, Field End Bridge, Mattinson's Bridge and Oldhall

*'A heron wings
slowly away . . .'*

Bridge. It is often edged with neatly layered field hedges and sometimes shadowed by ash or larch. A heron wings slowly away after feeding at the side of the brown water. Moorhens, equally busy on land or water, fly noisily upstream as an intrusive kestrel disturbs their nest-building. Each reach of the canal has its pair of swans.

Continue towards Crooklands, where snowdrops grow in great profusion below the road bridge. Leave the towpath by a squeeze stile on the right, just before the bridge. Turn left and then left again to cross the bridge. Turn left once more onto the A65 and cross to walk in front of the Crooklands Hotel. Take the signposted track on the far right of the hotel to walk down Bobbin Mill Lane.

Step out between the dwellings, pass through a grassy area where cars are repaired and then cross a pasture with the Peasey Beck flowing noisily to the right. Look right to the church on St Gregory's Hill. Climb the stile to the left of the gate and continue beside the pretty beck, now dropping downhill in a series of white-topped falls. Pass through the metal gate and another stile close to a weir. Climb the next stile beside the gate and turn left to walk on a raised track. The river makes a loop here, coming close to Kaker Mill.

The track ends at a narrow lane. Look right to see the attractive curving Challonhall Bridge over the beck and then turn left and walk up the hedged lane to Endmoor. Walk ahead along Enyeat Road, pass Calvert Antiques on the right, cross the A65 and take the footpath signposted Field End. As you climb the steepish slope, look right to the Howgills.

A magnificent view of the Lakeland mountains awaits you at the top of the hill. Nearer lies Whitbarrow Scar, with each crevice and hollow revealed in the bright wintry sunshine. Descend from the top, bearing slightly left and cross a stile in the corner of the pasture. Cross the track to Stubb Farm and take the footpath opposite, signposted Field End once more. (Make sure you take the correct path as there are several.)

Climb the slope, pass through a waymarked gate and strike diagonally left to another waymarked stile. Turn right and follow a muddy cart-track. Continue where it veers to the left, enjoying the magnificent views. At the waymarked gate walk ahead across the pasture to a stone stile in the facing wall. Turn right onto a narrow reinforced hedged lane. Pass Low Commonmire and follow Commonmire Lane as it bears left, where a snipe feeds in the muddy hedge bottom.

The lane drops gently downhill and swings to the left. Here take the narrow path through the larch trees, signposted Stainton. The path leads to the side of the canal. Turn right and walk to the end. Cross the stile on the right. Walk up a slope, keeping to the right of a bridge and take a very narrow squeeze stile in the wall on the left. Walk down the steps and continue through a larch copse.

Follow the signpost directions at the end of this small stretch of path, passing through a small area of scrub, to a stile. Beyond, cross a pasture, bearing right to a signposted stile, onto a narrow road. Turn left and cross the bridge over St Sunday's Beck. Look for the flood holes on either side of the arch. Pass through the dwellings to your car.

'. . . snowdrops -grow in great profusion'

Church of St Michael and All Angels, Beetham

6: Crooklands to Holme

Distance:	10 miles
Time:	5 hours
Parking:	On the B6385 by Crooklands Bridge
Terrain:	Easy walking all the way
Map:	Pathfinder 627 SD 48/58 Milnthorpe
	Pathfinder 637 SD 56/57 Burton-in-Kendal & Caton

This circular walk, taking in more of the Lancaster Canal, starts at Crooklands, where you left the canal on the last walk, and saves the glories of the towpath until the return journey.

If travelling north along the A65 turn left over Crooklands Bridge and then immediately right. On the right side of the B6385, beside the hedge, is a wide verge for safe parking. Ignore the tantalising glimpse of the canal and return to the bridge. Do not cross but continue along the narrow lane, signposted Milton, that runs parallel with the canal.

Follow the hedged lane as it swings right. Keep beside the Peasey Beck on its way to join the River Bela. Elms and larches hang over the water. Below the hedge flower common mallow, field scabious, ragwort and pink campion.

Where the road divides, take the left turn, signposted Milton Mill, and continue in the signposted direction of Wath Sutton. Pass by the three-storey building with its outbuildings dated 1563 and then

Garth Bridge

below the more modern A590 to the lane ahead. Turn right and walk up the narrow hedged lane, which is banked with wild flowers. Where the road widens look for the footpath on the left, signposted Kidside.

Walk beside the thorn hedge on the right, passing through two gates, and then take the stile in the hedge, half-way along the next pasture. Turn left and walk two sides of the field, where in spring cowslips grow, to a stone stile beside a gate. Beyond, cut left across the corner of the field to a stile over the fence, giving access to the

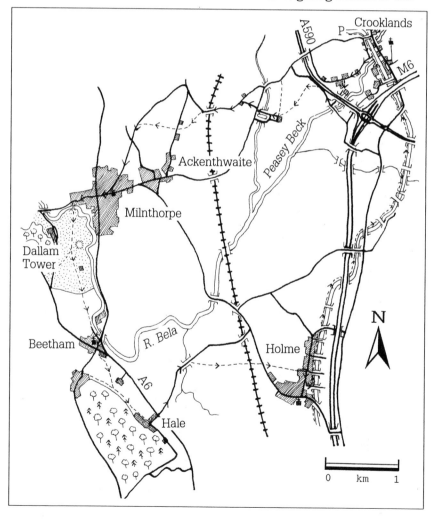

track to Kidside Farm which you have just passed on your left. Turn right and walk to the B6385, which you cross to take the signposted stile opposite.

Beyond, strike right across the buttercup pasture to a stile beneath an ash. From here there are grand views of Ingleborough, the Howgills and the Lakeland hills. Head down left to a gate onto a narrow road and continue left past Lower Rowell (built in 1790). Continue across the railway bridge and past Higher Rowell (with its pump) to a gap stile, signposted Ackenthwaite, on the left. Climb the slope below a yew tree and continue along the stiled way, keeping the hedge to the right. Beyond the cottage ahead, turn right to walk a ginnel to the road.

Turn left and walk on to a stile on the right, signposted Heversham, opposite High Crag Yeat. Walk straight ahead to two gates, side by side. Pass through the one on the right and continue up the stiled way to Haverflatts Lane, with a good view of Whitbarrow Scar. Turn left and stroll this gloriously peaceful, narrow way. At the crossroads, continue in the same direction and walk downhill into Milnthorpe.

Cross the A6 and walk ahead, along the B5282, until you reach the kissing gates to Dallam Park, on the left. Cross the buttressed bridge over the River Bela, built in 1730, and walk up the grassy slopes, keeping Dallam Tower to the right. The gracious house, built in 1720, replaces an earlier building on this perfect site. Drop down the slope to pass between a row of huge horsechestnuts where the famous herd of fallow deer graze and shelduck fly down and join them on the pastures. Climb the slope ahead to the signposted stile over a ha-ha, a ditch that keeps stock in or out without spoiling the view with a fence.

Walk downhill to cross a ladder stile and walk on along the lane, behind Beetham

Fallow deer & Deer House, Dallam

34

' . . . inquisitive swans come close . . .

Mill and the Corn Mill, into Beetham, stride the busy A6. Bear right to pass in front of the church of St Michael and All Angels, still with Saxon stones to be found within its fabric. Continue up the hill and turn left opposite Bela Cottage. Walk ahead to the signposted footpath on the right. The way passes behind the houses to another footpath sign. This directs you diagonally left to the far left corner of the pasture, behind Beetham Hall. This fourteenth-century pele tower, now part of a farm, was built for shelter against the skirmishing Scots.

Continue along the stiled way, passing through some delightful limestone woodland, to the linear village of Hale. At the road, turn left and walk to the A6. Cross with care and stride out along the narrow lane on the right of the King's Arms inn. Walk the lane to Pye's Bridge Farm and cross the bridge beyond. Look for the broken signpost on the right and pass through the right-hand gate. Walk up the slope, keeping the hedge to the left.

Keep in the same direction to cross a stile over the fence and another, immediately on the right. Walk ahead to the stile to the railway line. Cross with care and follow the well marked stiled way to the B6384. Cross the road and follow yet another waymarked stiled way into Holme. (Note the white painted stiles that take you to the right of the farm track.)

Turn right and walk along the road to pass the school. Turn left and follow a track that leads to a bridge over the canal. Do not cross but drop down left to the towpath. Turn left and step out along the gloriously easy-to-walk grassy way. Enjoy the summer flowers; the host of young mallards that bob about on the dark water; an inquisitive swan that comes close, hoping for food; the swallows and the grey wagtails that dart overhead and the coots and moorhens busy on the water's edge.

Cross the road on the edge of Holme to rejoin the towpath. As you come close to the M6, follow the footpath to the left, beside the motorway. Turn right to cross a bridge over the racing traffic and walk to the next canal bridge, Duke's, with steps on the right to the towpath. Turn left and walk on and on along the lovely waterway. Take care by the Canal Garage to pass under the M6 in order to regain the towpath (well-signposted) and then stroll onwards past banks of meadowsweet until you reach Crooklands Bridge and your car.

Scabious

36

Crag-bound ash on Hutton Roof limestone pavement

7: Holme to Saltermire Bridge via Hutton Roof

Distance:	10-11 miles
Time:	5 hours
Parking:	Near Holme
Terrain:	Easy walking all the way. Steady climb from Hutton Roof.
Map:	Pathfinder 637 SD 56/57 Burton-in-Kendal & Caton

Leave the M6 by the A65 at junction 36. Turn right at the roundabout 100 yards ahead onto the A6070. Take the third turn on the right, signposted Holme, to pass under the M6. Drive 200 yards to cross the culvert over the canal and park in one of the wide grass verges that lie on either side of the road.

Join the canal towpath, walking south along the wide grassy way. Notice the bridge you pass under is a skew bridge, built askew the canal. Enjoy the birds: the noisy mallards; the solicitous swans, caring for their large cygnets; the busy moorhens, which seem to spend as much time on land as on the water; and the swallows and house martins, which dive low over the canal, devouring insects in great quantities in preparation for migration.

Mill pond and workers' cottages, Holme Mills

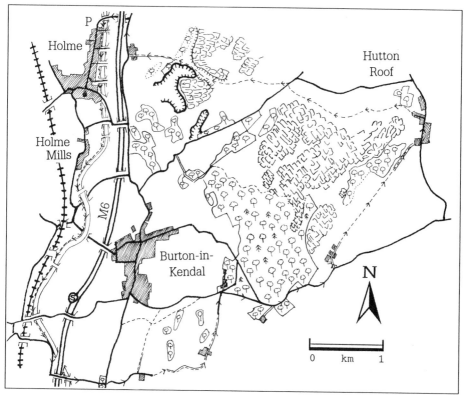

Beyond the seventh bridge look right to see Holme Mills, with its
mill pond and workers' cottages. The peaceful path is sometimes
lined with shady larches and deciduous trees but more generally
hedged. Hazel, hawthorn, rose, elder and honeysuckle are laden
with plenteous fruits. Purple loosestrife, scabious, bindweed,
hardheads and tansy brighten the verges.

After three miles the path comes to the side of the motorway. Pass
through the kissing gate and walk on along the road to cross
Saltermire Bridge over the roaring traffic. Thankfully, the noise is
soon left behind.

Look right beyond the bridge to see the highest of the eight
Tewitfield locks. Walk the hedged lane and follow it where it drops
downhill. Cross the A6070 and then walk on into the peaceful,
rolling countryside just over the border from Lancashire. Ignore the
first footpath sign and continue to Coat Green Farm. Take the right-
hand gate of two, to walk a short walled track. Continue beside the
wall on your left, where the track ends. There is little sign of a path
but the wall leads you to a small bridge, almost lost in undergrowth,
over a stream.

Walk ahead to a gate in the wall in front of you. Continue onwards to join a farm track which becomes very muddy as you near Dalton Old Hall Farm. Pass between the farm buildings and the farmhouse and walk along the access track. Look for the pump, standing forlornly in pasture to the right. When you reach the road, turn right and walk uphill, with deciduous woodland to the left. Continue along the road for just under a mile. There are magnificent views of Ingleborough and Whernside. Just beyond the first right turn, take the farm track on the left that leads to Crag House Farm.

'the pump standing forlornly in pasture'

Near the farmhouse take the right fork to pass between the outbuildings. Bear left beyond the farmhouse to walk a grassy track beyond a gate. Pass through the next gate and then negotiate the derelict stile in the far left corner of the next pasture. It stands below several ash trees. Continue ahead. To the left rise the limestone skirts of Hutton Roof Crags and to the right are grand views of Barbon Low Fell and Middleton Fell.

Cross a tiny stream, where water mint grows in profusion, by a small stone footbridge. Walk ahead to climb a stone stepped stile into Park Wood Nature Reserve. This was bought by the Nature Conservancy Council in 1979. In the limestone woodland, to the left, grow ash, hazel, field maple and wych-elm. Walk to the gate ahead to join a wide cart-track, along which you continue. Beyond the next gate the track passes through a yard to the village of Hutton Roof.

Turn left and walk through the pretty village. Look for the old smithy, with a plaque that says it is 252 1/2 miles to London! Turn left into a walled track, signposted Holme via Hutton Roof, part of the Limestone Link way. Beyond the gate the path contours the slope and then climbs steadily and unrelentingly, through bracken, to the edge of the Crags. Suddenly it seems as if you are on the roof of Cumbria, not just Hutton Roof. The view is stupendous, stretching from the Howgills, through the Lakeland hills to Black Combe. Enjoy this breathtaking airy walk.

The path swings left, up a slope, and then continues right as a wide grassy highway. Step out along the path as it passes through woodland where juniper, guelder rose, hazel and ash are laden with fruit. Look for agrimony, harebells and honeysuckle in flower. And then Morecambe Bay lies ahead, blue and sparkling in the afternoon sunshine. Stroll downhill to a ladder stile to a narrow road. Cross and pass through the gate opposite.

Follow the grassy track as it swings left to pass a waymark. Cross a cart-track and walk on to a ladder stile. Beyond, stride across the pasture to another gate. Walk along the pleasing waymarked path, past clints and grykes below Holmepark Fell. Overhead a kestrel quarters the pasture. Head down the good track where a flock of young long-tailed tits flit through the branches of ash.

Walk the gated track to the A6070. Turn right and take the next left turn to pass under the motorway to rejoin your car.

Harebells and agrimony

Tewitfield Locks

8: Tewitfield Locks to Carnforth

Distance:	10-11 miles
Time:	6 hours
Parking:	Tewitfield Inn
Terrain:	Easy walking all the way. Farm tracks muddy in winter.
Map:	Pathfinder 637 SD 56/57 Burton-in-Kendal & Caton and SD 37/47 Grange-over-Sands

P ark in the large, signposted car park beside the Tewitfield Inn, on the A6070 just to the east of the M6. Walk forward to the edge of the canal, then bear right to pass beside the M6 and below the A6070 road bridge. Step out along the wide, well-kept grassy towpath beside the Tewitfield lock flight.

Here eight locks, now without their gates, raised the Lancaster Canal 75 feet in $1/2$ a mile. A notice, placed on an intact pair of gates set beside the canal, says that these were the only locks on the 57 miles of canal between Preston and Kendal and that they were in use from 1819 to 1942. The pair of gates would have stood at the top of the lock, with another pair at the bottom. Long balance beams were attached to each gate and were used to open and close them.

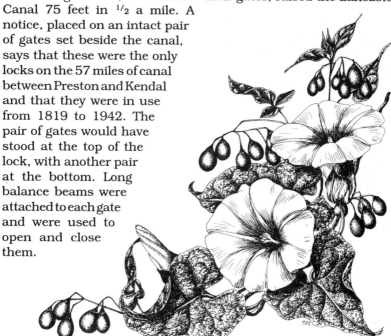

43

Convolvulus and woody nightshade berries

In September 1992 Lancaster Canal Trust workers began to restore the disused locks to the point where all that would be needed to get them working again would be the addition of gates and paddle gear.

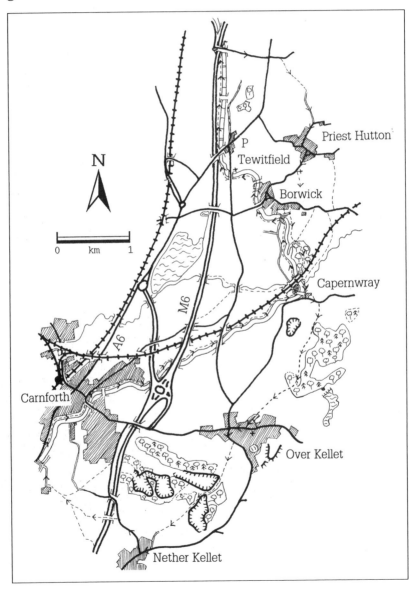

Where the towpath ends, obstructed by the M6, pass through a gate and turn right to cross Saltermire Bridge over the waterway. Walk ahead along the quiet country lane, where pink convolvulus grows and woody nightshade bears large red, glass-like berries. Cross the A6070 and walk ahead. Pass through the second farm gate on the right and stride across the pasture to a gate in the far left corner. Beyond, pass through another gate immediately left. Again walk right, across the pasture, to a gate in the far right corner. Walk ahead to a gate that gives access to an overgrown track which is walled and hedged.

Turn right at the end of the track and walk into Priest Hutton, with its delightful houses around the village green. Leave the green by the signposted Borwick road to walk past the memorial hall and St Mary's Church. Next to the church a signposted footpath, approached by stone steps, directs you right to Borwick. Here make a short diversion right to see the turreted Borwick Hall, an Elizabethan house built around 1590 for a Kendal clothier named Robert Bindloss.

Retrace your steps to pass the footpath exit and walk on to take a footpath on the right, signposted Hodgson's Bridge. Bridges south of Tewitfield are numbered and this is bridge 134. Step out along a

Hodgson's Bridge

45

ginnel, and then a path, to a stile. Cross a meadow to another stile. A charming Rennie bridge lies to the right. Here you may wish to shorten the walk by crossing the bridge and returning right along the towpath to Tewitfield.

To continue the walk turn left beyond the last stile and follow the track as it swings right to a gate. Carry on walking ahead, passing through a stile in a wire fence. Beyond the next stile, on the edge of a wood, turn right to walk a wide path through deciduous trees. To the left lies an old limestone quarry, now lost under trees and low-growing vegetation. The path brings you to the side of the Capernwray Canal Arm. It was constructed to link the quarry with the canal.

Continue beside the water to where it joins the main canal and walk on past mallards and coots idling in the sun. Look right to see the sturdy viaduct carrying the railway before the latter crosses above the canal over bridge 133, beneath which you pass. A few yards beyond you cross the Keer aqueduct, a single span of 43 feet carrying the canal 35 feet above the River Keer, constructed in 1797.

Leave the towpath before the next bridge, 131, and pass left through Capernwray Old Hall Farm and left again along the road. A flock of young starlings hunts for grubs in a pasture beside the road and then rises as one to settle, chattering noisily, on overhead wires. Turn right into Old Hall Caravan Park access road and then right once more through a metal gate opposite a gnarled oak.

Walk on, through gated pastures, keeping parallel with the edge of Kellet Park Wood. Follow a narrow path as it bears right to pass through a copse of oaks to a metal stile hidden by lush vegetation. Coal tits hunt among the oak leaves for insects and a tree creeper climbs along the lower side of a branch, it too seeking prey. Beyond the metal stile walk straight ahead to a stile between two gates and continue on to a stile leading to a track that leads in turn into Over Kellet by a small village green. Turn right and walk to a second green.

Turn left to leave the attractive village, with its views of Morecambe Bay and Warton Crag, along the road signposted Nether Kellet. Pass the Eagle's Head inn and cross to the right side of the road. Take the signposted steps that climb steeply to a kissing gate leading to a pasture. Beyond, walk ahead to cross a metal stile and continue to the left corner of the field. To the left you can see Ingleborough and Pen-y-ghent, their tops intermittently veiled in mist.

Climb a stile beneath a huge ash into a young larch plantation. From now onwards the path is fenced and waymarked as it passes between four great holes in the ground, all part of Over Kellet quarries. Here ragwort, harebells, wild mignonette and white deadnettle line the path. Look left to see the Ashton Memorial towering over Lancaster. A final gate leads into a hedged track where honeysuckle perfumes the way.

At the track end, walk along Laithbutts Lane to take the second right. This leads into Nether Kellet. Take the next right turn, signposted Carnforth, to walk towards the M6. Pass through a metal gate on the left, just before the motorway, to cross over the hurrying traffic, using a footbridge. Pass through the gate ahead and then walk to the far right corner to a stile. Take the gap stile on the other side of a grassy track and follow a path to a three-armed signpost. Over a hedge a highland bull, red-brown and very curly, scratches its back with its long horn.

Climb the ladder stile opposite the signpost and cross right to another into a farm track. Walk ahead to another signposted ladder stile. Cross the pasture, where highland cows look on with interest but do not move, to a gap stile by a gate. Turn right to walk away from Thwaite House Farm. This hedged track leads beneath horsechestnut trees - where a grey squirrel races through the branches - to bridge 127. Cross the waterway and turn right to take a gate on the right to the towpath.

Walk through Carnforth, with its marina, passing beneath bridge 128. Follow the path to pass beneath the M6 and then on to Kellet Lane Bridge, 130. Beyond, continue through the lovely rolling countryside. Much of the path is densely shaded by trees, summer flowers border the way, ducks and swans come to the edge of the water curious about passers-by, and swallows and house martins hawk flies before departing for warmer climes.

Pass under bridge 131, seen earlier. Continue ahead, this time retracing your earlier route on the west bank of the canal. Look for the Capernwray Arm, bridge, 134, and an interesting view of Borwick Hall just before you reach bridge 135. Continue to Tewitfield and turn right just beyond the canal basin (the limit for cruising) to regain the car park.

Plaque on the now disused lock gates

Canal bridge at Hest Bank

9: South of Carnforth to Hest Bank

Distance:	6½ miles
Time:	3 hours
Parking:	Southern edge of Carnforth. Lay-by by Bridge 127.
Terrain:	Easy walking all the way
Map:	Landranger 97 Kendal to Morecambe

This walk takes you through pastures to continue along the shore of Morecambe Bay, returning beside the canal. For some of the time you walk within sight of the A6 and for much of the time within sound of it, but the birds busily continue with nesting, unperturbed. Flowers bedeck the way.

Park by bridge 127 at the southern edge of Carnforth on the A6. If you are travelling south, in the direction of Lancaster, the lay-by, part of the old road, lies on your left, next to the canal. Walk back 50 yards to take a left turn, Crag Bank Road, signposted Crag Bank and the Shore. Walk ahead to cross a railway bridge. Continue to where the road makes a sharp right turn. Turn left to cross a stile into a hedged cart-track lined with jack-by-the-hedge and wild arum. Willow warblers and hedge sparrows sing from the depths of hawthorn bushes laden with creamy blossoms.

Cross the stile to the left of a gate and continue ahead. In the reed-fringed dyke to the right a reed warbler chatters continuously. Cross a small bridge and walk on beside the drainage dyke, where kingcups grow. Oystercatchers feed in the pastures. Cross the next stile and then follow the rising track to a stile beside a gate. This gives access to a hedged grassy track lined with cow parsley, pink campion, violets and bluebells. At the end of the track, cross the stile to a lane and turn right. From here look back for a good view of Warton Crag.

Walk along the lane, passing through a caravan site, and continue beyond a gate to pass through the

Willow warblers sing from depths of hawthorn bushes

49

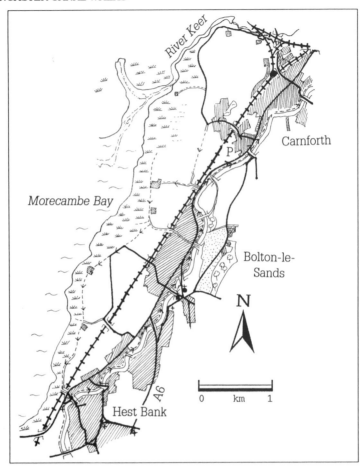

yard of Bolton Holmes Farm. At the end of the lane a gate leads to the pebbled shore of extensive marshland edging the sands of Morecambe Bay. Turn left to walk the pebbles to join a lane that continues along the edge of the saltings. The short turf is dotted with mats of sea thrift and here skylarks fill the air with their sweet songs. Continue past Wild Duck Hall, where a sparrow hawk hunts for prey, flying low along a hedgerow.

Bear right along a path over the marsh, just beyond a pebbled track used by cocklers and their tractors, keeping close to a fence on the left. Climb the steps onto a splendid embankment from where there is a grand view over the bay. Stride along this breezy, grassy raised way to Red Bank Farm. Drop down to the shore and walk

. . . a sparrow-hawk hunts for prey

ahead. Out on the wide stretches of sand, enthusiasts race in their sand yachts and horse riders canter far out into the bay.

Continue along the marsh above the sands and below sandstone cliffs covered with trees in soft green foliage. Take the continuing track that passes in front of two mock Tudor houses and continue to Hest Bank station. Use the two notice boards to help you identify the seashore birds and the mountains that stretch from Black Combe to the Howgills.

Cross the level crossing and then Marine Drive to walk up Station Road. Cross The Crescent and take the steps onto the towpath. Turn left to walk towards Carnforth. Just before bridge 118 small boys fish for bream and carp. Beyond bridge 119 a pair of swans have built a high straw nest on the far bank. Here several grey cygnets sunbathe and two remain under the pen's wings, unconcerned by a water vole swimming through the reeds close by.

Walk on past Hatlex Swing Bridge, 120, and then beneath bridge 121. The latter is not a Rennie bridge but a sturdy affair built to carry the A6. Continue under bridges 122, 123 and 124. Beyond, an oranged tipped butterfly flits among the bluebells. Look for a moorhen nesting in the ivy that clasps a substantial hawthorn tree.

'. . . an orange tipped butterfly flits among the bluebells'

After obtaining food the female first climbs the canal bank, then the slightly leaning trunk of the tree, to reach her nest. To continue foraging she climbs to the top of the tree and then drops down into the water, her olive-green legs dangling as she descends.

Beyond Bolton Cinder Ovens Bridge, 125, fish jump and buttercups line the grassy edge of the towpath. Enjoy the grand views over Warton Sands. Continue beneath bridge 126 and walk to the lay-by by bridge 127, where you parked your car.

51

Turning pool

10: Hest Bank to the start of the Lune Aqueduct

Distance:	5¹/₂ miles
Time:	3 hours
Parking:	Near level crossing, Hest Bank
Terrain:	Easy walking all the way, but can be exceedingly muddy in parts after prolonged rain
Map:	Landranger 97 Kendal to Morecambe

Park in the large car park on the shore side of the level crossing at Hest Bank, approached by the A5105. Pause to enjoy the large flocks of waders that feed as the tide recedes. Re-cross the railway line and the A road. Head up Station Road towards the canal, where you can see boats moored. Cross The Crescent to attain the towpath, and turn right. The Hest Bank section of the canal is the closest the waterway comes to the sea.

After passing under bridge 117 you very quickly move out into the gentle rolling Lancashire countryside. Gulls dip low over the water and call raucously as they go. Continue along the hedged towpath, where blue tits chatter in the thorn bushes, to walk below bridge 116. Note bridge 115, called Blind Lane Bridge, because you will cross it on your return. Once there were stables here for the canal horses, but all trace of buildings seems to have disappeared.

Stroll on along the towpath. Just before Belmont Bridge, 114, is a large pool edged with willows and alders. Here boats were turned round. Just beyond

' . . .
Oystercatchers
feed noisily in
the pastures'

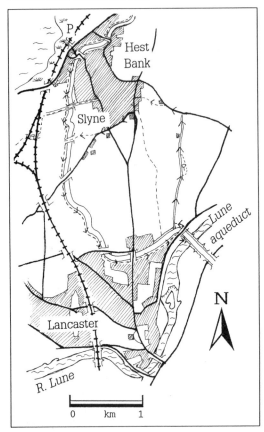

bridge 113 a flock of oystercatchers feeds noisily in the pastures on the opposite bank. Curlews fly over the canal, bulky white-rumped birds uttering their wild, haunting whistle.

Continue beneath Foley Bridge, 112, and bridge 111. Hedging largely conceals buildings on the outskirts of Lancaster. Stride on to pass beneath bridge 110 which has been widened to carry the A6. Pass below bridge 109 and continue past fishermen hoping to catch pike.

Pass below the Halton road bridge, 108, and past the small basin on the far side. Walk on to see the magnificent Lune Aqueduct. Built of stone, designed by John Rennie and opened in 1797, it is 660 feet long and carries the canal 51 feet above the River Lune.

Do not cross the aqueduct but return to bridge 108 and ascend a path on the left to reach the road. Turn right to cross the bridge and take the unsignposted footpath, on the left of the road, passing through a gap in the hedge; the stone steps that once gave access to the path have fallen out of place and are of no use to the walker.

Continue ahead, gently climbing, keeping beside the hedge with the canal on your left. Climb the stile into a reinforced track called by local people Black Castle Lane. Turn right and walk the grand hedged track, most likely a Roman road. A legend describes how in the last century some young folk were walking the track when they heard the thunder of horses' feet. They jumped into the hedge out of the way, but though they watched no horses went by. They assumed they had heard the ghosts of Roman soldiers.

54

Gulls (black-headed)

On reaching a metalled road, turn left and walk downhill for 300 yards. Turn left to pass through a gate just before a small farmhouse with a stone marked 1646. In a couple of yards pass through the next gate and turn right. Strike across the pasture towards a caravan site and climb the awkward stile, in a hedge, into the site. Walk ahead to another stile in the left corner of the caravan field. Continue ahead. Beyond the gap on the left walk on, keeping the hedge to the left. Drop downhill to a stile to a wide grassy track between the houses of the village of Slyne.

A kissing gate gives access to the A6, which you cross. Turn left and then right into Throstle Grove, signposted Hest Bank Lane. On the corner of the road notice the old cattle pound, now a pleasantly paved area with seats. Outside the wall stand stocks.

Head down the Grove, following the lane as it bears left. At the crossroads, continue ahead along Hasty Brow road. Turn right to walk a narrow lane. Turn left through a white gate on the left just before the entrance gate to a large house. Beyond the white gate is the wide, grassy hedge-lined Blind Lane that leads to Blind Lane Bridge, 115, which you cross. Take the stile on the right to regain the towpath.

Retrace your outward route, passing beneath bridges 116 and 117. Beyond, look for the exit from the towpath, signposted the Village Centre and the Shore, to return to your car.

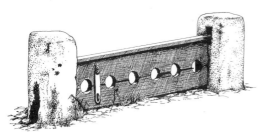

'Outside the wall stand stocks'

Lune Aqueduct, Lancaster

11: Lune Aqueduct to Aldcliffe returning along the Lune

Distance:	8 miles
Time:	4 hours
Parking:	Near bridge 109, outskirts of Lancaster
Terrain:	Easy walking all the way. If the tide is high use the Lancashire Coastal Way footpath, a few yards to the right, rather than keeping to the edge of the water.
Map:	Landranger 97 Kendal to Morecambe

L eave the A6 by any turning signposted Halton. Park as close as you can to bridge 109 on the north-eastern outskirts of Lancaster. This bridge is just wide enough for only one car to pass at a time.

Drop down the stone steps to the towpath and walk right, towards the magnificent Lune Aqueduct.

Pass beneath the overhead power lines and bridge 108. The aqueduct, 107,

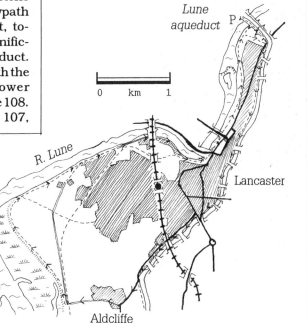

57

lies ahead. Supported by five huge masonry arches, it carries the Lancaster Canal for 660 feet, 51 feet above the River Lune. It took five years to build and was opened for use in 1797. Its architect, of course, was John Rennie. Pause on the aqueduct to enjoy the extensive view downstream to Lancaster.

Notice at the end of the bridge a flight of steps on the right, signposted the Lune Estuary path. You will climb these steps later to complete the circular walk. Look right to see the Ashton memorial, the castle and the cathedral. To the left lies the golf course. Continue beneath a metal bridge and on to bridge 105. Now you are in the centre of Lancaster, with dwellings on both banks. The towpath is hedged, and in the branches house sparrows, blue tits and blackbirds chatter.

Head along the path to pass below bridge 104 and look left to see a dry dock on the far bank. Then comes Dry Dock Bridge, number 103, a wrought-iron footbridge. A host of mallards swim towards the path, hoping to be fed. Continue past several tall mills, where once cotton was produced, now converted to homes or offices. Close to Moor Lane Bridge, 102, is a pleasing sitting area with a pergola dedicated to the industrialist Thomas Tredgold. Here anglers fish for perch and roach and reminisce on the days when the mills were in use.

Pass under bridge 102 and walk on to bridge number 101, which has the name of another industrialist, Joseph Clayton, 1876, emblazoned on it. This is a skew bridge, with the stonework of the arch going aslant over the water. Overshadowing the bridge and the canal is St Peter's Roman Catholic cathedral. Once beyond bridge 100 the towpath ceases and you climb steps to cross the bridge. You

Lancaster - waterfront

Peregrine falcon

continue along the opposite bank past bars and restaurants with picnic tables beside the water.

Stride on along the path, the water shadowed by Scots pines, to pass below the massive road bridge, number 99. Beyond, continue beneath a footbridge to come to a public house, The Water Witch, originally stables for the horses that pulled the canal boats. Opposite are two large basins where boats are moored. Continue to the splendid turnover bridge, 98, where, without uncoupling the horses from the boats, they could be backed to the other bank. Cross the bridge to rejoin the towpath. On the opposite bank lies a restored, but roofless, building where boats were once repaired. Notice the end of the building, which is skewed for ease of access. Walk on to pass beneath bridge 97, which carries the railway. Bridge 96 is an iron footbridge. Haverbreaks Bridge, 95, is unusual for not having a keystone. Beyond, to the right, lie open pastures. The towpath here is railed and you continue to the end of the fencing.

Leave the towpath and continue along the gently sloping hill to the village of Aldcliffe. Where the road swings left stride ahead. Walk past the houses and out into the open countryside where redshanks fly overhead, giving their hunting call. Continue to the end of the road, cross the stile and turn right, following the signpost directions for New Quay Road via Foreshore.

Walk the raised embankment, with flat marshland stretching away to the estuary. Curlews call and move restlessly upstream. A large flock of lapwings rises as one and heads north. Dozens of swans feed in the tidal gutters. Oystercatchers pipe and probe the grassy sward for food. As the swans move upstream a lesser white-fronted goose is seen feeding among the larger birds. Beyond, on the roots of a dead tree, sits a peregrine - its presence probably accounts for the restlessness of the curlews and lapwings. In the ash and hawthorn hedge on the right a mixed flock of chaffinches and goldfinches flits ahead as you walk.

Follow the foreshore path as it swings right and comes close to the surging water of the Lune. Stride on to cross two stiles, keeping beside the Lune until the path ends at the quay. From here, continue along the road ahead to pass various mill buildings and a huge viaduct, with a new span in the middle, over the river. Do not cross but head on past Lancaster Maritime Museum.

Just before the next viaduct, cross the road and take the footpath leading off right, signposted The Castle and Priory. Follow the stepped footpath as it winds uphill to the disused railway. Turn left to cross the viaduct. This is a grand high level walk from which you can look down on the city of Lancaster and the stately River Lune. At the road turn right to follow the footpath right to an underpass below the road. At the other end, turn left to the path beside the Lune to continue upstream. The path passes through the riverside park, with good views of the Priory and the Castle on their hill.

Pass beneath the balustraded five-arched bridge and continue along the track of the little North-Western Railway that once ran between Morecambe and Skipton. The way now continues through silver birch and thorn bushes. Keep beside the river to see the magnificent weir where boys balance along the structure, hunting for dabs. Walk on to see the aqueduct ahead. Take the long flight of steps, noted earlier, up to the towpath. Turn left and cross the huge bridge. Stride on below bridge 108 to the steps before bridge 109. At the top turn left to regain your car.

'A white-fronted goose is seen feeding among the larger swans'

View over Lune Estuary -with oystercatchers wheeling above

12: Galgate to Aldcliffe, returning along the coastal path beside the River Lune

Distance:	7 miles
Time:	4 hours - this is a walk not to be hurried
Parking:	Conder Green picnic site
Terrain:	Easy walking all the way
Map:	Pathfinder 659 SD 45/55 Galgate & Dolphinholme and Landranger 97 Kendal to Morecambe

To reach the Conder Green picnic site and car park, turn off the A588, Lancaster to Cockerham road, by the Stork Hotel at Conder Green, and drive 400 yards to the site. Walk back along the narrow road, with the River Conder to your right, to pass in front of The Stork. Turn left and almost immediately right, opposite Keeper's Cottage.

Walk down the lane, where bindweed has large white flowers, to a tall ladder stile on the left, just before Webster's Farm, opposite an unfenced road coming in on your right. Walk ahead, past the back of the farm, to pass through a gate. Continue to the far right corner to another gate leading to a stiled stone footbridge over a ditch. Turn left and walk along the edge of Crow Wood to a stile. Stride on,

Kingfisher

keeping to the right of the hedge, to a metal ladder stile. Continue ahead to climb the stone stepped stile to Parkside Farm.

Pass between the farm buildings and step out onto a track continuing in the same direction. Turn right to pass through a gate, just before an electricity pylon. Turn left and, keeping the hedge to your left, walk to the metal stile in the corner of the pasture. Beyond strike right across the pasture to a metal stile which gives access to a narrow path through Forerigg Wood.

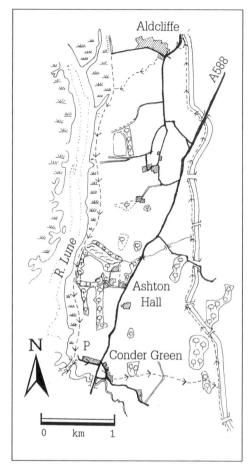

Leave the wood by a similar stile and turn right to another stile. Beyond strike left across the meadow to a stile leading to the towpath of the canal. Turn left and begin a splendid walk along one of the loveliest stretches of the canal.

In autumn you are serenaded almost continually by robins, which have started to sing again after their late summer silence. Each bush seems to have its resident redbreast. You pass beneath six bridges of varying height and shape, designed by John Rennie: New Park, 89, Ashton Park, 90, Brantbeck, 91, Burrow Beck, 92, Carr Lane, 93, and Deep Cutting Bridge, 94. Mallards and swans come close to the towpath expecting to be fed. Moorhens feed and squabble and court along the banks. Long tailed tits flit through the hawthorns along the edge of the path and mistle thrushes fly down from the tree tops to bathe and splash in the sun-warmed water.

Bridge 91 is the start of the Deep Cutting, a 1 1/2-mile cutting made to eliminate the need for locks. Beyond the bridge the towpath carries you above Burrow Beck, which is siphoned noisily below. The water hurries on, the banks of the stream bedecked with Indian balsam. Notice Carr Lane Bridge, 93, has a railed area in the centre of its parapet.

Look for a kingfisher winging its way towards Lancaster, its plumage an electric blue in the sunshine. It settles on a branch close to the still water and then flies onwards, keeping just above the surface. Here the steep slopes of the cutting are clad with riotously coloured deciduous trees. Stroll on along the path until you reach the road to Aldcliffe. Here turn sharp left and walk the lane to the edge of the village.

Take the first right turn, just before the village sign, and drop down the hill. Very soon the houses are left behind. Continue along the hedged lane, where blackberries, elderberries, hips, haws and wild bryony are laden with fruits. Turn left to walk the signposted

Robin singing

Lancashire Coastal Way, which follows the route of a dismantled railway that carried passengers and goods from Glasson Dock to Lancaster.

Enjoy this hedged path, which passes Aldcliffe Marsh, the haunt of curlews and oystercatchers. Huge flocks of green plovers whirl

and dive low over the silvery water. Tansy flowers along the verge together with pink clover, harebells and yarrow. The path comes closer to the water's edge before passing between high banks where guelder rose, red in leaf and berry, brightens the way.

A heron flies across the wide estuary, calling raucously, and settles on the mud. Across the sparkling river you can see the boats of Glasson Dock. Continue beneath a smoke-stained bridge and on along the delightful way to regain the car park.

Hips and blackberries

Signpost at the junction of canals

13: Conder Green Picnic Site via the canal near Galgate

Distance:	4¹/₂ miles
Time:	2 hours
Parking:	Conder Green picnic site
Terrain:	Easy walking all the way
Map:	Pathfinder 659 SD 45/55 Galgate and Dolphinholme

Start walking as for Walk 12. On reaching the towpath, turn right and walk beside the quiet water. In late March wood anemones, red dead-nettle, coltsfoot and celandines flourish below the thorn hedge, where both rose and hawthorn are in leaf. Pass below Ellel Hall Bridge, 88, and continue to the Conder aqueduct, 87. Lean over to see the stream hurrying beneath the low arch. Look for the buttresses and curving walls.

Continue along the path, where elder and willow are now in leaf. Beyond bridge 86 is the Galgate marina. Walk on to pass the lock-keeper's cottage to the junction of the Glasson Dock branch with the main waterway, where you turn right. Stride the lovely path beside the canal as it passes through the peaceful countryside. The River Conder flows to your right. Look for the Swaledale and Suffolk sheep grazing with their lambs below the sycamores of a small copse on the far bank close to the Second Lock bridge.

Head on along the

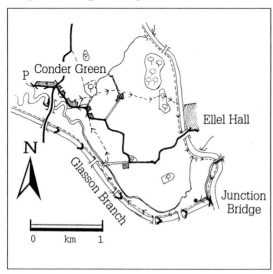

66

Snipe path towards the railed Third Lock bridge. Before the bridge water from the River Conder enters the canal. A large number of handsome shelduck feed and a hare, long-legged and long-eared, races over the pasture. Continue onwards to pass under bridge 4.

Step out until you reach the gate on the right just before Bailey Bridge, 5. Pass through and walk ahead to cross a drainage ditch by an earth bridge. Continue ahead to a railed footbridge, where gorse bushes are laden with golden blossoms, to cross the River Conder. Walk diagonally left over a pasture to a gate through which you pass.

Beyond, walk ahead, keeping to the left of a hedge. Overhead wings a heron on its way to fish in the Conder. At the end of the hedge, walk on across the pasture, where peewits feed. They rise frequently, circle and then dive headlong back to the marshy field. A plank enables you to cross the stream at the field boundary. Here a pair of snipe rise from the muddy ooze and fly off, low and fast. Pass through the gap stile and head towards Berry's farm, walking beside the hedge on your right.

At the road, turn left and continue to Webster's farm. Where the road curves left, walk on along the narrow lane to the A588. Turn left and then right beyond the Stork Hotel and stride the narrow lane to return to the picnic site.

Wood anemones

Glasson Dock

14: Conder Green via Glasson Dock

Distance:	4¹/₂ miles
Time:	2 hours
Parking:	Conder Green picnic site
Terrain:	Easy walking all the way. Some tracks can be muddy after rain
Map:	Pathfinder 659 SD 45/55 Galgate & Dolphinholme

Park in the car park of the Conder Green picnic site, on the site of the old Conder Green station (see Walk 12). Return to the hotel and walk south along the A road to cross Conder Bridge. In the tidal gutters of the river shelduck feed and redshanks and oystercatchers probe the mud. Continue to Thurnham Bridge, 6, over the canal and climb the stile on the left to drop down a slope to the towpath. Turn right to pass under bridge 6. Red admiral butterflies flit along the path. Meadowsweet and willowherb bedeck the verge with late kingcups still flowering in the damper areas. Coots and moorhens proudly escort their second brood close to the water's edge.

Stroll along this glorious path beside the still water and pass

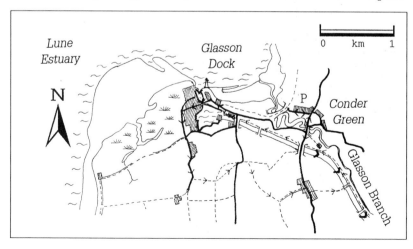

under Brick Kiln Bridge, 7, and Brows Bridge, a skew bridge, 8. Walk past Christ Church, Glasson with its fine bell tower, built 14 years after the canal. Follow the signpost directions for Glasson Basin and Dock. To the right lie the golden sands of the Lune Estuary.

Turn left to cross the swing bridge to the other part of Glasson. Look left to see the canal basin, used as a marina, and right the dock, where ocean going boats are loaded. Glasson Dock was developed when the River Lune silted up in the 1780s and ships were unable to reach St George's Quay, Lancaster. The

Red Admiral on meadowsweet

Glasson branch of the canal was opened in 1826. Ships took coal to Cornwall, bringing back china clay. Timber, wood pulp and iron ore all arrived at the dock.

Walk up Tithebarn Hill and sit on the seat at the top. Look out over the rich pastures of the marshes, where Masham ewes and their large, fat lambs snooze in the warm sunshine. Across the estuary lie Sunderland Point and Overton. They look deceptively close but are in fact a mile away. Before you continue your walk, spend some time in the walled area on the corner and use the indicator panels to name the mountains and hills.

Stride along the lane as it swings left and passes between dense

Glasson Dock Church

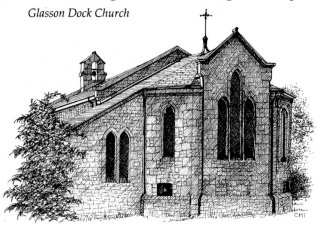

hedgerows. Where it swings left again, walk ahead along Dobs Lane. Honeysuckle, in full flower, trails over the hedges. Walk past the Old Glasson farm, with its two extremely tall silo towers and, beyond, stride out into the lush marshland. At the signposted cattle-grid, turn left to walk a cart-track where wrens scold from the hedgerow and water mint flowers in the drainage ditch on the right. Hares race across the pastures and green plovers perform their erratic aerial dances.

Honeysuckle

Continue to the end of the track and bear diagonally left across the pasture to a gate to the road. Turn left and follow the road as it bends right. Just before it bends left again, walk ahead on a cart-track and follow the rough, muddy track as it bears right. Step out where the track crosses the flat pastures and continue where it swings left, to pass the large black silo of Aspley Farm on the left.

Pass through a gate and walk up an even muddier track to the road. Turn right past an old cottage and almost immediately turn left before a house with a bed and breakfast sign.

Look across the meadows to the right to see the Gothic façade of Thurnham Hall, where once lived the Dalton family, some of whom were buried in the church at Glasson. Blackthorn bushes line the track, their white blossoms replaced by small green sloes. Where the track ends, bear slightly left across the pasture to Bailey Bridge, 5, which has white railings. Cross the bridge, turn right and walk to a gate onto the towpath. Turn right to pass beneath Bailey Bridge, and continue along the towpath, where more butterflies settle on foxgloves growing along the stony edge of the way.

Walk past a lock with a tall wooden bridge for access to the far side and a weir to take away surplus water. Continue in front of

Shelduck

Thurnham Mill, once a water-powered corn mill. Today it is being converted into a hotel and restaurant. Notice the water race and the nearby lock. Walk towards bridge 6, where it and its reflection create a perfect oval. Climb to the stile and turn right and then left in front of The Stork to rejoin your car.

Double Bridge

15: Cockerham to Thurnham

Distance:	5 miles
Time:	2¹/₂ hours
Parking:	Close to the parish hall at Cockerham
Terrain:	Easy walking all the way except for some very muddy pastures and one very muddy lane
Map:	Pathfinder 659 SD 45/55 Galgate & Dolphinholme

The quiet village of Cockerham lies not very far from the sea, whence come wild winds to bend the trees and buffet the tower of St Michael's church. The walk starts here, taking you across the lush pastures to the side of the canal, continuing beside the Glasson branch, returning past Thurnham Hall and through peaceful farmland to Cockerham.

Park close to the parish hall on the B5272. Walk north to pass in front of the Manor Inn and continue to a turning on the right, Willey Lane (spelt Willy on the O.S. map). This is a bridlepath signposted Ellel Grange, 1¹/₂ miles. The reinforced, neatly hedged track leads out onto pastures, and is bordered with celandines, dog's mercury and the large glossy leaves of wild arum. Follow the track

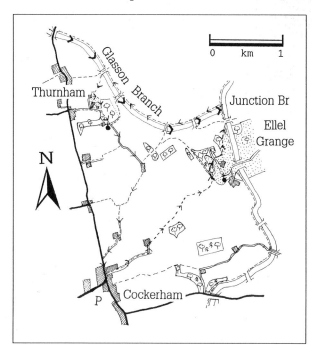

Turnover Bridge

as it swings left towards a farm called Up Town and then right just before the dwelling.

The track, in winter, ends in a very muddy area. Beyond this bear left to pass through a gate behind an electricity pylon. From the gate strike diagonally right across the rolling pasture, keeping a small wood to the right, to a gate in the boundary fence. Beyond, walk on, diagonally right, across the corner of the pasture, to pass through a farm gate. If it is locked you will have to climb over to continue on the right of way. From the pastures curlews call and lambs hurry to the comforting sides of their dams.

Drop down the gentle slope to a footbridge and walk ahead to another. Here a green woodpecker flies off from a dead elm. Beyond the footbridge, swing left to walk beside a deciduous wood carpeted with the bright green leaves of bluebells. Take the first gate into a wide grassy area between two sections of a wood. Walk in front of Ellel Grange, a fine Italianate building with towers and columns, and past a horsechestnut in flower, to pass through a gate to the right of Home Farm. Notice the ship on the weather vane above the dwelling.

A gate opposite gives access to pleasing parkland. Continue to the gate ahead, keeping a hedge and fence to the left. Beyond, walk diagonally left to come close to Double Bridge, 85, over the canal. It is double the width of other canal bridges and has a wall along the middle that serves as the boundary between two farms. Notice its keystone and the glorious reflection in the still water. There is no access to the tantalising towpath here and the way continues above the canal, close to the bordering thorn hedge, until reaching a squeeze stile. This gives passage to the path and the junction of the canal with Glasson branch. A few yards ahead is Junction Bridge, 1, on the branch waterway.

Cross the cobbled turnover bridge, 1, and turn left to walk the towpath, which is edged with primroses, in the direction of Glasson basin. Pass four locks, all with weirs and high wooden bridges. Beyond locks 2, 3 and 4 stands a pleasing stone bridge named after each lock beneath which you pass. Just before the fifth bridge, Bailey Bridge, cross a stile on the right of the path and walk parallel with the canal. Climb a ladder stile to cross the bridge.

Once over, walk ahead to a gate and stile in the opposite hedge. Follow a wide, wet, grassy area between two tall hedges. Then, where the way ends, walk ahead over pasture, towards Thurnham Hall. Cross a narrow stream, bear left into deciduous woodland and then right to walk in front of the Gothic fronted hall. The way was difficult to find at the time of writing because of the building work being done in converting the hall and grounds into a timeshare complex.

On reaching the lane turn left to walk past the glorious catholic church of St Thomas and

Green woodpecker on dead elm

St Elizabeth (1847-48). Notice the large ornate tomb to the side of the church. Stride on along the reinforced lane and follow it as it swings left and uphill to Cock Hall Farm. Walk ahead through the outbuildings and then turn left and immediately right to a gate at the edge of the

Primroses

farmyard, into a very wet pasture. Strike right across the sodden ground, where shelduck graze, to a footbridge over a drainage gutter.

Continue in the same direction to a gate in the far corner of the next pasture that gives access to an extremely muddy lane. After 50 yards it swings left and it is possible to walk a grassy verge to avoid the worst of the mire. Follow this track to Batty Hill Farm and on to the A588. Turn left to return to Cockerham.

Ellel Bridge

16: Cockerham to Forton including a long walk along the canal

Distance:	7¹/₂ miles
Time:	4 hours
Parking:	Close to the parish hall at Cockerham
Terrain:	Easy walking all the way. Some footpaths and cart-tracks can be very muddy after rain
Map:	Pathfinder 659 SD 45/55 Galgate and Dolphinholme

Park as for Walk 15. Take the signposteded footpath to the north side of the parish hall. This is a wide reinforced track that leads to St Michael's church, which has a solid ashlar-built Perpendicular tower with the remainder built in 1910 by the architects Austin and Paley.

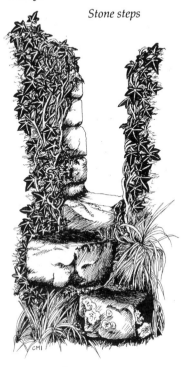

Stone steps

Leave by the kissing gate beyond the church, and walk ahead, bearing slightly left to reach the boundary hedge to the left of a bungalow. Walk left along the hedge, where goldfinches, blue tits, robins, blackbirds and chaffinches congregate, finding shelter from a February gale. Climb the stile in the hedge at the end of a row of trees, and bear diagonally left to a tractor bridge over a ditch. Look for a long-legged hare racing across the flat pastureland.

Continue left, keeping to the right of a thorn hedge, to a wooden footbridge over a tributary stream of the River Cocker. Turn right to walk to the edge of the Cocker and then continue left to walk beside the hurrying river, which is deeply channelled between steeply sloping banks. A pair of swans swim gracefully, the banks protecting them

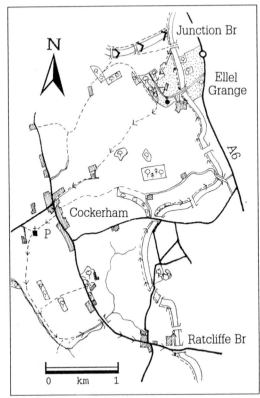

from the worst of the winds. A flock of skylarks feeds in the pastures and then fly off into the gale.

Cross the stile close to the water's edge and continue past Little Crimbles Farm, remaining on the same side of the Cocker. Walk on along the gated way to the attractive Burns Bridge, which is sturdily constructed in stone. Here shelduck feed in the pastures. Do not cross but turn left to walk the access track to Crookhey Farm. The track bears left and then right through the buildings to the B5272. Turn right and cross Crookall Bridge. Walk along the quiet hedged lane where snowdrops brighten dark hollows and honeysuckle is in leaf. Continue to a junction. Where the road, Park Lane, swings right, continue ahead along the minor road to the white-railed canal bridge, Ratcliffe Bridge, 75.

To reach the towpath bear right before the bridge. Then walk left below it to continue along a glorious stretch of the waterway which is hedged with hawthorn and elder. The canal is bridged by two more white-railed bridges, Corless and Smiths, 76 and 77. The next bridge you pass beneath is Stony Lane Bridge, 78 and the next, 79, carries the road to Cockerham.

A great spotted woodpecker climbs on a branch of an alder. It then flies across the canal and is joined by another, and the two birds ascend an ash, probing the bark as they go. Continue along the graceful curving waterway, shaded now by deciduous trees on either bank. Harts tongue fern spreads its leaves almost to the water's edge, on the far bank. Pass below Richmond Bridge, 80, and walk on to Potters Brook Bridge, 81.

Greater spotted woodpecker

Stroll the towpath to pass over a stream by a small aqueduct, bridge 82, and continue to Hay Carr Bridge, 83, which is shadowed by graceful beech trees. In the pastures beyond the bridge Masham sheep, with curly wool, black noses and black eyes, call to their frolicking black-faced and black-legged lambs. Ahead, to the left, towering over woodland, is the spire of St Mary's church in the grounds of Ellel Grange. The canal passes through the grounds of the grange. Look left to see a small lake close to the towpath. And then Ellel Grange Bridge, 84, with its classical balustrade, comes into view, flanked by beech and Scots pine. The fine bridge was built to match the grandeur of the grange, with its imposing towers and doorway flanked by columns.

Continue along the towpath into pastureland and then pass below Double Bridge, 85, mentioned in Walk 15. The way continues through a small cutting to Junction Bridge over the Glasson branch. Do not cross but look for the gap stile on the left. Pass through and walk diagonally left, heading towards Ellel Grange. Climb the sloping pasture and pass through a gate in the boundary fence. Walk ahead, keeping to the left of a fence and a hedge, to a gate to a track which you cross. Pass through the gate opposite and continue ahead to walk a grassy gap between two areas of woodland to a gate.

Beyond the gate, bear diagonally left to a wooden footbridge with white painted rails - easily missed, hidden as it is by vegetation. Climb uphill to a similar wooden footbridge. Ascend the slope ahead to a gate in the top left corner. If the gate is locked, you will have to climb over to continue on the right of way. Bear left to pass through a wicket gate. Continue left, aiming for the nearest pylon, passing beside a pond on your right. Continue on your way by the gate at the foot of the pylon.

Walk diagonally left towards a farm track that leads to Up Town Farm. Just before the farm turn left and walk a hedged cart-track, Willey Lane, where wild arum and snowdrops grow below thorn bushes. Follow the track as it swings right and continue as it gently begins to climb. On reaching the A588, turn left to return to your car.

Viaduct over River Wyre

17: Forton to Scorton

Distance:	5¹/₂ miles
Time:	2-3 hours
Parking:	Lay-by by Ratcliffe Bridge, 75
Terrain:	Easy walking all the way
Map:	Pathfinder 659 SD 45/55 Galgate & Dolphinholme and 668 SD 44/54 Garstang

Drive south from Cockerham along Main Street. Where the road swings sharply right and becomes Park Lane, continue ahead to park in a lay-by close to Ratcliffe Bridge, 75. Park carefully so that you do not obstruct access to the farm track beyond. Climb up the bank to the towpath and walk right to pass moored boats. Along the bank grow horsetails, each cone-shaped spore capsule supported by a ribbed stem with whorls of spiky leaves. Coltsfoot abounds, and sycamore and oaks line the banks of this delightful stretch of the canal.

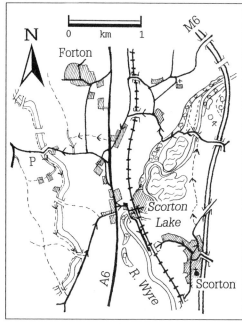

Pass beneath the railed Cartmels Bridge, 74, and walk on past a large bed of primroses close to a milestone. Green plovers feed in an adjoining field. Just before Cabus Bridge, 73, leave the towpath by a wooden gate on your right by Greaves Farm. Continue, to cross the bridge (73), and walk to Cabus Nook Lane.

Turn left and walk to the A6, which you cross. Head along the lane opposite, to the left of the phone box, and walk until you can see the dramatic viaduct over the River Wyre. Beneath the arches, the hurrying river white-topped and boiling, drops over a weir. Goat willows, heavy with golden catkins, lean over the water.

Cross the river by the metal Wyre Bridge and continue along the lane, with the railway now above to your left. Pass under the railway bridge and walk into Scorton. Wander around this charming village, which is hidden among trees below the motorway. How many people, speeding along the M6, have any idea of the gem that lies below? Look for the row of old cottages and the remains of a doubling woollen mill.

Turn left in the centre of the

Pair of bullfinches

village and continue past the houses to a signposted footpath, on the left, just before a bridge over the M6. Follow the footpath through trees to cross Park Brook. Continue where it swings right and is fenced. Cross back over the brook on a sod-covered bridge to climb a stile. Turn left and continue upstream. Cross another footbridge and walk to a stile beside a gate. Continue ahead, keeping to the left of a corrugated iron shed.

As you walk ahead, look left to see the attractive tree-fringed Scorton Lake, where tufted duck idle on the still water. Go over the next stile and continue past alders, laden with catkins. The next stile you cross leads to a fenced path. Walk along it to a waymarked stile and footbridge. Immediately ahead lies the fast-flowing River Wyre, at a point just above its wide loop to the west. It then continues west of Scorton Lake before passing beneath the viaduct seen earlier on the walk.

'tufted duck idle on the still water'

Turn right to walk a track to a stile. Beyond is a lane where you turn left to cross Cleveley Bridge over the Wyre.

Walk on to pass on the left Cleveleymere, from where comes the calls of ducks. Continue along the delightful wooded lane, where a pair of bullfinches whisper "whib, whib" quietly to each other and graceful long-tailed tits flit constantly through the branches of a thorn hedge. Ascend the hill, which is lined with pure white flowers of wild strawberry, to pass Cleveley Bank Farm.

Beyond the farm follow the lane as it swings left. Here the banks are bright with greater stitchwort and ground ivy. Cross the railway bridge and walk on to Hollin Lane, which you cross, and then walk left. After $^1/_4$ of a mile, turn right opposite a dwelling called Grey Cot into a short reinforced track that passes in front of the New Holly public house to the side of the A6. Cross and continue ahead to a stile behind the bus shelter.

Stride ahead along the stiled way to cross Winder Lane to take another signposted footpath continuing in the same direction. Climb the next stile and then head for the gap stile to a farm track in front of a red brick house. Turn left and walk the track past Nicholson's Farm to the lane. Turn right and walk the $^1/_4$ of a mile to Ratcliffe Bridge, 75.

Horsetails and coltsfoot

83

Canal boat and Winmarleigh Hall with Bowland Fells behind

18: Ford Green to Cabus Nook

Distance:	7 miles
Time:	3-4 hours
Parking:	Near Ford Green Bridge
Terrain:	Easy walking all the way
Map:	Pathfinder 668 SD 44/54 Garstang

L eave the A6 at Garstang by Croston Road. Turn right onto Nateby
Crossing Lane and almost immediately turn left in the direction
of the hamlet of Ford Green. Park in one of several grassy lay-bys on
either side of the Ford Green Bridge, 67, over the canal.

Walk down onto the towpath and head south. The grassy way is
a delight to walk and the greening hawthorn bushes hide many a
small bird, searching busily for a nest site. Hopeful fishermen cast
for perch, bream and roach.

Continue on beneath beech, ash and sycamore laden with
flowers. From be-
yond the trees come
the calls of curlews
feeding in the
pastures of Nateby
Hall Farm. Climb to
the right of Nateby
Hall Bridge, 66, and
turn right to walk
beneath a row of
limes. Bear left,
following the track
between the out-
buildings of the farm.
Continue ahead
along the cart-track.
Turn right at the
waymark just be-
yond a small clump
of trees, 50 yards
beyond the farm.

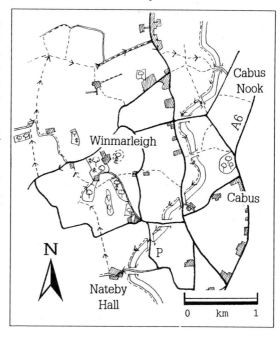

85

Follow the yellow arrows across the pasture to a footbridge over Lee Brook. Walk ahead to a stile set in a hawthorn hedge onto Whitters Lane. Look ahead to see Winmarleigh Hall, standing red-bricked and gracious among its deciduous woodland. This was once the home of the Patten family and is now part of Lancashire College of Agriculture.

Take the signposted footpath slightly to the left on the other side of the lane and cross to a stile set in the boundary wall ahead. A pair of hares race across the pasture, lowering their ears flat against their heads. Walk diagonally left to a stile to the right of a copse. Beyond, turn right and walk along the edge of woodland behind the college. Follow the track as it swings left and passes through a yard containing building materials and machinery. Pass in front of Gift Hall to Church Lane.

Blackthorn

Turn left and walk the quiet lane, passing the access track to Throstle Nest Farm. Here in a damp pasture five herons stand, well-spaced, seeming to enjoy the spring sunshine, unworried by the black-headed gulls that wheel and dive about them.

Turn right beyond the long straight dyke (Lee Brook) and walk to

the stile in the corner of the hedgerow ahead. Continue beside the dyke, where redshanks feed and pied wagtails strut along its muddy edges. Walk past Old Hall Wood and then across a pasture to a stile in the hedge opposite. Turn right onto a wide lane edged with blackthorn bushes adorned with white blossom. Where the track swings right to Throstle Nest, turn left and continue over the wide flat marshland beside the brook.

Redshanks feeding

On reaching Crawley's Dyke, turn right through a gap beside the gate into a track called Thorough Way.

Walk along this rough, grassy track - which was probably used for the removal of peats from the mosses - between tall hedges beneath which grow shirtbuttons, kingcups and milkmaids. Young calves, just let out from winter housing, race and frisk about the meadows beyond the trees, curious about anything that moves.

At Park Lane, turn right and walk 20 yards to the Patten Arms. Turn left into the car park and walk beside the fence on the left to the footbridge in the corner, over Park Lane Brook. Walk up the slope and continue ahead, passing to the right of a pool among trees. Strike right to a stile half-way along the hedge and continue in the same direction to a gate. Beyond the gate walk ahead, keeping the fence to the right, to the right-hand corner of the pasture. Turn right along a gated farm track to Cabus Nook Farm. Pass through the farm buildings, following the track as it swings left to a gate to the towpath.

Turn right and pass under bridge 73. Along this stretch of the waterway boats of all types are moored to the far bank, including two attractive converted long boats.

Walk along the glorious way to pass beneath bridge 72 and Winmarleigh Bridge, 71. From this stretch of the towpath look left across to the hills of Bowland. Continue beside the water to walk below Davis Bridge, 70, which carries a footpath from Park Lane to Fowler Hill Lane.

From here the canal curves to the east for a short distance and then to the west to pass below bridge 69, over which runs the B5272. Continue along the towpath below Bell's Bridge, 68, to walk on to return to Ford Green Bridge.

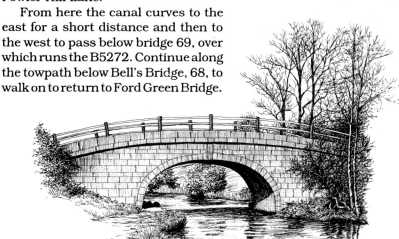

Winmarleigh Bridge, Garstang

On top of the Wyre Aqueduct

19: Garstang to Ford Green and Catterall

Distance:	8¹/₂ miles
Time:	5 hours
Parking:	Close to the leisure centre in Garstang
Terrain:	Easy, level walking all the way.
Map:	Pathfinder 668 SD 44/54 Garstang

Return from the large free car park to the road in front of the toilets, turn right to pass The Wheatsheaf and continue to a small roundabout. Here follow the signpost directions for the canal basin. Cross bridge 62 by its footbridge and then cross the road, Kepple Lane, to a short footpath that leads to the towpath. Turn left and pass under bridge 62.

Coltsfoot in flower brightens the verges as you walk the peaceful path. Look right to see the snow-topped Bowland Fells. Continue ahead to a point where you can view three bridges at the same time. The first is a striking white bridge, carrying a huge pipe, built in 1927 by the Fylde Water Board; this is bridge 63A and carries water from Barnacre Reservoir to Blackpool and its surrounds. The second, bridge 63B carrying the A6, has a balustrade. Beyond the third, 64, a traditional canal bridge supporting Nateby Crossing Lane, lies the delightful Lancashire countryside.

Stride the towpath until you reach the brick abutments (all that remains) of bridge 65. Before it was demolished it carried the "Pilling Pig", the name given to the Garstang-Knott End Railway. Look for the splendid row of beeches on the far bank. From pastures to the left come the haunting calls of curlews. Pairs of oystercatchers

Greenhalgh Castle

fly overhead and then settle to feed before moving restlessly to the next field. Beneath beech beside the towpath grows a carpet of celandines in flower. Follow the canal as it curves and comes to Nateby Hall Bridge, 66.

Take the stone steps just before the white railed bridge. Turn left and walk the access track towards Nateby Hall. Follow it as it curves left and passes between farm buildings. At the footpath sign pointing right, take the stone footbridge on the left and climb the stile beyond. Turn right and walk to a boundary hedge where you turn left to walk past a copse on your right. Continue to a concrete ladder stile which once gave access to the dismantled railway - look right to see part of the embankment. Continue through a copse with a pond surrounded with celandines to a stile to a pasture. Here all the mule ewes have sturdy triplet lambs.

Walk ahead, keeping a hedge to the left. Turn right onto a concrete track and after 50 yards turn left at the end of the trees.

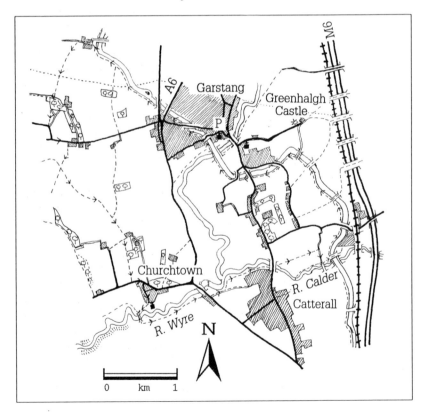

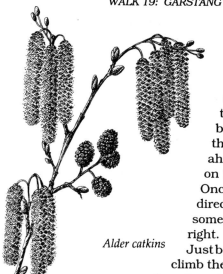

Alder catkins

Continue ahead to cross the pasture to a white stile leading to Kilcrash Lane. Turn left and walk ahead to Longmoor Lane, which you cross. Turn left and walk towards some houses. Just before the first dwelling climb the stile on the right and walk ahead, keeping beside the fence on the left to a stile on your left. Once over it, continue in the same direction, now with the hedge and some splendid ash trees to your right.

Just before the corner of the pasture, climb the barred fence - the only place where there is no barbed wire. Beyond, turn left and then strike right across the pasture to a stile. Beyond, turn left and walk to the end of the hedge. Turn left to cross a sturdy footbridge provided by Lancashire County Council. Look for the primroses in flower in the sheltered hedge bottom.

Turn right and follow the hedge to the next footbridge. Beyond, continue with the hedge to your left to the next footbridge. Pass beside a small pond where willows grow and the green spears of reeds are emerging. Bear slightly diagonally right across a pasture, keeping a stone barn to your right, to a farm track. Stride the good track, which runs to the right of Hall Farm. Where the track swings right pass through the double gates on the left, where you turn right to walk the access track. To your left, surrounded by trees, stands Kirkland Hall, once the home of the Butler family.

The track ends at Ainspool Lane, which you cross. Turn left and take the first turning on the right, signposted Churchtown. Continue past the market cross, and walk on to visit St Helen's church, sometimes called the Cathedral of the Fylde. Parts of the church date from the thirteenth century, its tower from the fifteenth. Look for the magnificent seventeenth-century wall paintings in the chapel.

Leave by the gate at the far end of the churchyard and cross the pasture to an elegant, stiled suspension bridge over the River Wyre. Climb the stile immediately ahead and continue ahead over a small pasture to a stile to the left of a squeeze stile. To the right stands

Catterall Hall. Climb the stile on the left and walk ahead along a raised track, the river flowing to your left but hidden from view by its steep banks. Ahead in the distance lie the Bleasdale Moors. Continue along the gated way. In the pasture to the right red dead-nettle grows in great profusion and on the alders, which line the riverbank, golden catkins sway in the breeze.

At the track end, turn right and walk for 50 yards to a short path that leads left to the A6, which you cross. Walk ahead for 200 yards along a signposted bridleway. Turn left just beyond a single-storeyed red-brick building to pick up a cart-track that runs upstream beside the Wyre. Take the stile and turn right just before the confluence of the River Calder and the Wyre and walk a footpath, keeping beside a hawthorn hedge on your right. Climb a ladder stile close to the river and continue to Calder Bridge on the B6430. Cross the road, turn left to cross the bridge and then take the signposted footpath on your right.

Walk the stiled footpath, keeping close to the hedge on your left. On reaching a cart-track, turn right and walk on, following the hedged track as it swings left. Catterall Bridge, 53, is 150 yards along. To reach the towpath take the gap stile on the right just before the bridge and turn left to pass below. Beyond is the Catterall basin.

Stroll the towpath to pass below Ray Lane Bridge, 54, where mallard pairs swim close together. Continue below bridge 55 and look ahead for your first view of the ruins of Greenhalgh Castle high on its hill. The Earl of Derby built the four-towered castle in 1490. The Parliamentarians badly damaged this Royalist stronghold in 1645, during the Civil War.

Continue on to pass below bridge 56, which has a deep balustrade. At bridge 57 Suffolk ewes crowd, waiting to be fed. Overhead peewits twist and dive, displaying to their mates. Walk on for a closer view of the ruins. Follow the towpath as the canal swings in a wide westerly curve to pass below bridges 58, 59 and 60. Look for the milestone on the next stretch, with 17 miles to Preston on one side of the stone and 13 to Lancaster on the other.

And then you come to the Wyre Aqueduct, where the canal is carried 34 feet on a single arch above the River Wyre. Descend the wooden steps to the bank of the river for a good view of the huge buttresses and the graceful curving arch. Return to the towpath and continue past the Garstang Basin, where coots and geese swim, overlooked by The Old Tithe Barn, which houses a small canal museum. Walk on to Kepple Lane Bridge, 62. Strike up the short path before the bridge and turn right to return to Garstang.

Walmsley Bridge

93

20: Catterall via Claughton-on-Brock

Distance:	7¹/₂ miles
Time:	3-4 hours
Parking:	Catterall, close to the B6430
Terrain:	Easy walking all the way
Map:	Pathfinder 668 SD 44/54 Garstang

Walk along the road to Calder Bridge and take the signposted footpath to the east side of the bridge (see Walk 19). Walk the stiled footpath, keeping close to the hedge on your left. On reaching a cart-track, turn right and continue, following the blackthorn-hedged track as it swings left. Kingcups grow in bright golden clumps close to a stream and wild parsley flowers in profusion along the way to Catterall Bridge, 53.

Cross the bridge and turn right to walk 50 yards beside the canal

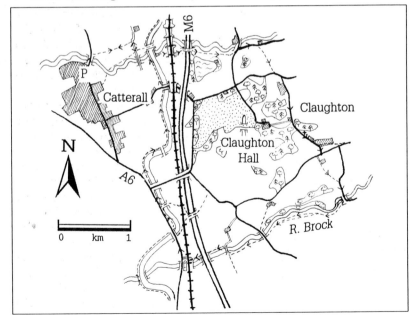

to Calder Aqueduct, 52. Below, a siphon takes the River Calder beneath the canal. Turn left and strike diagonally right to a stile beside a gate. Continue ahead to pass under a railway bridge. Head towards the footbridge over the M6, which you cross. To the right is a large pond, with a solitary fisherman.

Stride ahead across a pasture, keeping the pond and a hedge to your right. Here curlews call as they fly over their nesting sites then utter their bubbling calls as they descend to their nests. To the left flows the alder-lined River Calder, where a dipper flies upstream.

Pass through a stile by a gate and walk a few yards along a track to a lane. Turn left and then right, following the signpost directions for Bleasdale. From the thorn bushes along the lane comes the fluted song of a thrush, and beyond ewes tend their new-born lambs. Wild strawberry and greater stitchwort brighten the hedgerow banks.

Take the second farm gate on the right and walk to the stile ahead. Continue ahead, with the hedge to your left, to a stile behind a huge oak in the corner of the field. Continue ahead to the next stile beside a gate which gives access to a track to Crabtree Nook. Pass through two huge metal gates and follow the track to a lane. Turn left and walk on to pass Cross House and its pond.

Strike on along the quiet country lane until you reach St Thomas's church, Claughton-on-Brock. Enter to see the ornate gilt decorations and the bas relief pictures of the Stations of the Cross. Continue onwards to pass the school and its pond, and follow the lane as it swings right. At the next junction, cross the road and turn right. After two steps, turn left into a cart-track to walk to the right of a small farmhouse. Beyond the dwelling look for a stile on the right into a pasture.

Kingcups

Turn left and walk beside the hedge on the left to a stile, which you cross. Swing left to a footbridge over a stream to the lane. Turn right and walk on to cross Walmsley Bridge over the River Brock. Turn right to pass through a gate and follow a path that keeps parallel with the river. Follow the stiled way, from where you have glimpses of the tree-lined river, racing over its deeply fissured bed. At a large, wide pasture, with the

95

river away to the right, stride ahead to a stile close to some large houses. The path continues at the foot of their gardens and close to the river. Follow the waymarks to a road and New Bridge.

Cross the road and continue along a signposted metalled track beside the Brock. Tall trees border the river and from these come the calls of a willow warbler and a chiff-chaff. At the waymarked footbridge, cross to the opposite bank and continue downstream where wood anemones and butterbur flower.

Pass below the M6 and continue along the track to the railway line, which you cross with due care. Head on along the track to the A6. Turn

Milestone

right and walk for ¼ of a mile to Green Man Bridge, 47. The steps to the canal towpath descend on the far side of the bridge, on the right side. Head north where the edge of the path is bordered with forget-me-nots.

Continue beneath bridges 48 and 49. Beyond, the canal continues with a graceful curve. Here the delicate moschatel flowers along the verge. Pass under the high-arched bridge 50. Both banks support pleasant woodland. Close to Stubbins Bridge, 51, a hare races across the pastures. Kingcups grow along the banks of this quiet stretch of water.

Walk on to cross the Calder Aqueduct. Then, just before bridge 53, take the short path on the left and pass through the gap stile onto the track taken earlier.

Turn left and follow the track as it swings right. Look for the gate on the left. Beyond, walk ahead, keeping to the left of the hedge, until you reach Calder Bridge and the village of Catterall.

*St Thomas's Church,
Claughton-on-Brock*

View of canal with moored barge

21: Around Brock

Distance:	5 miles
Time:	2-3 hours
Parking:	On the A6, north of Brock
Terrain:	Easy walking all the way
Map:	Pathfinder 668 SD 44/54 Garstang and SD 43/53 Preston (North) and Kirkham (Lancs)

Park close to the wide reinforced verge on the bridge over the River Brock. The verge lies on the A6, immediately south of the Dutton Forshaw showroom and north of the centre of the village of Brock. Look over the bridge to see the river, stained chocolate-brown, rage over a weir. It surges angrily, swollen with water from the fells above after a day of rain.

Walk north for 200 yards along the A6 to Green Man Bridge, 47. Cross the bridge and take the steps down to the towpath. Turn right to pass beneath and continue along the flower-bedecked path. Swallows fly low over the water, feasting on a myriad of midges. Quiet pastures stretch away on either side and it is grand to be away from the noise of the main road and the railway.

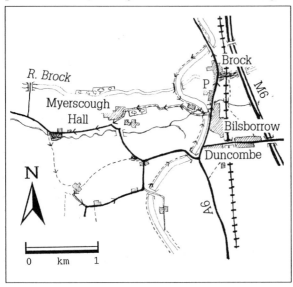

A heron stands motionless on the bank, watching the water for an unwary fish. When disturbed it flies off with a resounding squawk. Stride on past milk-maids, vetch, gipsywort and jack-by-the-hedge. Look for the character-istic mile-stones

Wild cherry blossom

along this stretch of the canal which give the distance from Preston and Garstang. These enabled the bargees to know when to rest their horses.

Cross the Brock Aqueduct, 46, a single span 60 feet long. Designed by John Rennie, it carries the canal 22 feet above the River Brock and was first used in 1797. Lean over the wall to see the hurrying river, shadowed by willows and lined with gorse loaded with bright yellow blossoms. Continue past a copse carpeted with bluebells. From the trees with pale emerging leaves comes the sweet song of willow warblers.

Walk beneath bridge 45 and climb the steps on the left. Turn left and walk the quiet lane, passing several dwellings. Head on along the way, where cowslips flower and cherry trees are in blossom. Continue past Crow Wood, which is floored with dark blue bluebells whose perfume wafts on the breeze. Follow the tracks as it swings left and then right to pass through the many buildings of Myerscough Hall, the College of Agriculture. The track finally swings left again to come to the road.

Turn right and walk for ¹/₂ a mile to pass Myerscough Lodge Farm on the left side of the road. Just beyond the farm take the unsignposted footpath also on the left side. Cross the sturdy stone footbridge over the Old River Brock and turn left to walk beside the beck. Cross the farm track and walk ahead, keeping to the side of the hedge on your right. Climb the stile over the fence to

'A heron stands motionless . . . '

cross a small stone footbridge beneath which flows a narrow stream. Walk ahead keeping the hedge to your left.

The indistinct path soon become a track, paved in places. This was the old road that linked Lodge Farm with Lee Farm, the cluster of buildings reached by following the track as it swings left. Walk ahead when the track leads to the barn to a gate onto the farm access road. Turn right and continue to a quiet lane. Turn left and walk the hedged way to pass Hallidays Farm. Look right to see Head Nook Bridge, 43.

Where the lane swings sharp left, turn right to walk a metalled track to the bridge. Beyond a gate on the left, steps lead down to the towpath. Turn left to stroll the towpath, where the canal curves gently to the east. Beyond Roebuck Bridge, 44, lies Owd Nell's Tavern, a thatched building, the centre of a small leisure complex. The towpath continues through Bilsborrow, where many colourful boats are moored.

Continue to the steps taken earlier just before bridge 45. Climb these and turn right to walk to the A6, which you cross with care. Turn left and walk the ¹/₄ mile to regain your car.

Canal boat

Hollowforth swing bridge

22: Carefoot to Hollowforth

Distance:	4¹/₂ miles
Time:	2-3 hours
Parking:	Near Carefoot
Terrain:	Easy walking all the way
Map:	Pathfinder 43/53 Preston (North) and Kirkham (Lancs)

Leave the A6 at the turning for Myerscough Agricultural College. Take the first turn left, at Carefoot, and drive the narrow country lane to where it turns sharp right. At this corner a gated track continues to Moon's Bridge, 36, and it is possible to park here for the start of the walk.

Walk to the gate on the left just before the bridge to descend steps to the towpath. Turn right to pass below the bridge and continue along a lovely stretch of the canal where linnets twitter from the top of the hawthorn hedge. After ¹/₄ of a mile look for the waymarked stile in the hedge. Beyond, bear diagonally left to a stile close to a tall ash tree half-way along the boundary wall. Continue in the same direction to the far left corner.

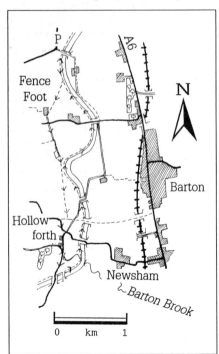

Climb the stile and walk to the signposted footbridge on the right which gives access to a farm track just left of Fence Foot Farm. Turn left and walk to the crossroads, then continue ahead along a reinforced track which is lined with bluebells and pink campion. At the end of the track walk on to cross a stile into a wide grassy way edged with hawthorns which are laden with tight white flower buds. Below the bushes, wild arum is now in flower. Curlews call from the pastures on either side.

Stride ahead to a wide turf bridge, and a gate, between two lovely tree-fringed pools from where willow warblers and wrens give their melodious calls. Carry on in the same direction to climb four more stiles. After the fourth, turn right and walk through milkmaids to a signposted footbridge to turn left into Eaves Lane.

Terns

At the T-junction, turn right into Hollowforth Lane.

As you stroll the quiet lane past Hollowforth Hall look for the colourful peacocks that strut about the grounds. Cross the bridge over New Mill Brook and walk onto Moon's Bridge, 36. The stile to the towpath is on the right, just before the bridge. Turn left to walk beneath the skew bridge and continue past moored boats to bridge 37, the white painted Hollowforth Swing Bridge.

Continue along the towpath to Hollowforth Aqueduct, 38. The bridge is railed and there is a way down to walk along its edge to descend to the side of Barton Brook. The aqueduct has three arches. The brook hurries under two. Under the third streams the overflow covered by a metal mesh, and carries the Newsham footpath.

Walk on along the towpath. Look for a heron, like a bent stick, patiently waiting for an unlucky fish. In the beech wood on the left wild garlic fills the air with its pungent aroma, but this does not deter a blackcap that sings from the depths

Footbridge, Fence Foot Farm

of a hawthorn bush. Pass under Hepgreave Bridge, 39, and continue on to Hankinson Bridge, 40. Beyond a pair of sandwich terns pause on fence posts and then fly gracefully overhead uttering their wild cries. They turn in mid air and drop down, almost horizontally, to the water before gliding up again and flying away down the waterway.

Stroll on along the towpath as the canal curves gracefully through the lovely spring countryside of Lancashire. Kingcups border the water and their rich gold is reflected in the still water. Pass below Park Head Bridge, 41, and White Horse Bridge, 42. Just beyond Head Nook Bridge, 43, take the steps on the left to return to your car.

Arum

Whinnyfield Bridge

23: Swillbrook to Woodplumpton

Distance:	3¹/₂ miles
Time:	1¹/₂ hours
Parking:	Close to Free Methodist Church, Crown Lane, Swillbrook
Terrain:	Easy walking all the way
Map:	Pathfinder SD 43/53 Preston (North) and Kirkham (Lancs)

Walk along Crown Lane, which runs to the left side of the church. Continue, to pass Crown Lane Farm, to a gate. Beyond walk on in the same direction, keeping to the right of the fence. Pass through the gate ahead, the gate replacing an earlier stile.

Keeping beside the hedge on the left, continue ahead through a pasture where curlews call and fly high over their nests. The right of way continues along a farm track and then crosses a wooden footbridge, in need of repair, over Woodplumpton Brook. Stride on along the continuing farm track to Whinnyfield Farm. Pass right through the outbuildings onto a narrow lane. Follow this as it swings right and enjoy the view ahead of the Bowland Fells. Then, where it turns right again, cross the stile on the left and stride across the

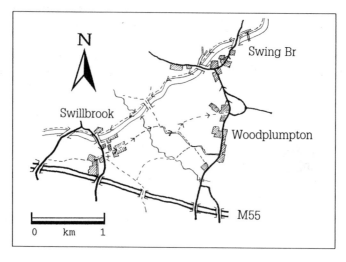

pasture to the hedge corner. Walk right, with the ditch and hedge to your left, to a plank bridge over the ditch.

Goldfinch

Climb the stile at the end of the plank, which gives access into a pasture where cows graze placidly. Cross the pasture, bearing slightly right to another plank over a dry ditch with a stile beyond it. Turn right and walk beside the hedge on your right, where grow several magnificent ferns, to a stile onto a narrow path which continues to a lane. Turn right and walk 30 yards to the B5411 where it passes through Woodplumpton.

Turn left and walk ¹/₄ of a mile to take a turn on the right, Hollowforth Lane. Buttercups grow in great profusion on either side of the quiet lane, which leads to Moon's Bridge, 36. Cross the skew bridge and take the stile on the left to reach the towpath. Stroll south to pass through more of Lancashire's peaceful pastures.

At Bell Fold Bridge, 35, you pass Woodplumpton Mill. Goldfinches twitter as they flit across the canal to trees on the opposite bank. Large leaves of water lily float on the still surface and kingcups brighten a dam corner of the bank. Continue to Whinnyfield Bridge, 34, a charming arch reflected in the glassy water below. Look for the large planks, freshly tarred, beside the bridge. These are for blocking a stretch of the canal when repairs are needed.

The towpath continues on, edged with bluebells, white

Bluebells, white deadnettle and ground ivy

107

dead-nettle, gipsywort and ground ivy. House martins race along the canal, shrieking as they catch flies. Walk on to pass the aqueduct over Woodplumpton Brook, 33 - here water from the canal slides over into an overflow and down to the brook. Stride on to pass a boatyard with a small shop. Just beyond is the Old Stables Cottage, now the Jolly Roger tea shop where they sell delicious bread and serve cream teas. Leave the towpath just after the old stables, where the horses that pulled the boats were housed, and before Swillbrook Bridge, 32.

Turn left to cross the bridge. Look over the parapet to see an attractive signpost giving distances along the canal. Continue along the road in the direction of the church to regain your car.

Signpost at Swillbrook Bridge

24: Swillbrook to Salwick

Distance:	7 miles
Time:	3-4 hours
Parking:	Close to Free Methodist Church, Crown Lane, Swillbrook
Terrain:	Easy walking, but the deep soil of Lancashire, which supports such healthy stock, holds much water after rain
Map:	Pathfinder SD 43/53 Preston (North) and Kirkham (Lancs)

Walk south along Crown Lane for a dozen yards and pass through a gate on the left into a pasture which is full of inquisitive heifers. Cross diagonally right to a stile in the far corner. Carry on through the large gap on your right and walk across the pasture to a footbridge over the M55.

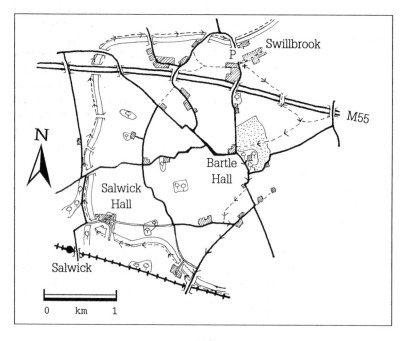

Continue over the hurrying traffic and at the foot of the far flight of steps walk ahead to a stile, ignoring the more obvious stile on the right. Stride ahead over a buttercup pasture to a gated track, which after rain can be very muddy. Continue along the waymarked track,

A hare . . . 'races across the pasture.'

which is lined with heavily berried hawthorns, and pass below a power line. Beyond the gate and stile turn right and pass through a kissing gate. Head on, with the hedge to the left, past more inquisitive heifers, to pass through a gap. Walk on to a footbridge in a hedgerow over a narrow ditch.

Continue ahead, keeping parallel to the wire fence on your left, to pass through a stile by a gate. Beyond, walk across pleasing parkland with well-placed oaks and horsechestnut trees. A hare with long ears laid back races across the pasture and lingering house martins glide overhead. Climb the waymarked stile beside the woodland of Bartle Hall and turn left into Rosemary Lane.

Walk ahead to turn left into Lea Lane to pass below huge beech and horsechestnut trees. Here the road is littered with a profusion of mast and conkers. Pass Bartle Hall, a country hotel, and walk on below more horsechestnuts. Ignore the left turn to Preston and carry on along this pleasing lane to pass the Sitting Goose pub and Ivy Farm. Take the signposted footpath on the right and walk ahead through sheep pastures. On reaching a hedge on your left, bear diagonally left to a stile in the far left corner of

Horse chestnuts and beech mast

Bridge with pointed parapets

the pasture.

Carry on, with a hedge to your left, and continue beside a drainage ditch, also to your left. At its end, bear very slightly left to walk ahead to a gate which gives access to a single track lane, where you turn left. At the lane end, turn right to walk the hedged road, where honeysuckle, woody nightshade, bramble and cleavers are laden with fruits. Cross bridge 22, with its curved parapets, turn left and drop down to the towpath. Turn left to walk beneath the bridge and out into the countryside.

Enjoy this glorious stretch of the towpath. Reeds, rushes and irises line the banks, their leaves tinged with gold. Mallards, coots and swallows abound and patient fishermen watch their lines. Pass below Ward's House Bridge, 23, with its pointed parapets. Beyond, white bindweed, white dead-nettle, silver weed, marsh woundwort and great willow-herb colour the verges. Salwick Hall Bridge, 24, has deeper parapets and beyond this bridge stands Salwick Hall.

Continue to pass below Wilson's Bridge, 25, where delightful reflections from the water flicker across the stonework. Beyond is Salwick Wharf, where several boats are moored. Follow the canal as it begins to curve north, the towpath taking you below large forest trees. Sunlight filtering through the leaves dapples the water.

Pass below an aqueduct and then look left to see the handsome Hand and Dagger pub. Salwick Bridge, 26, has deeper parapets and

112

here the towpath continues on through the pleasing countryside. Six Mile Bridge, 27, is another Rennie bridge with pointed parapets. From the ploughed field on the opposite bank a flock of green plovers take flight and cross to a pasture by the towpath.

And then you pass below the motorway and walk to Kellet's Bridge, 29, which has railed, curved parapets. Here there is another mooring. Roots Bridge, 30, has white railings on its pointed parapets. Beyond, a pair of swans swims across to the towpath, hoping to be fed. Pass below Stone Chimney Bridge, 31. Then Swillbrook Bridge, 32, comes into view and the circle is almost complete. Climb left up the far side of the bridge, turn left to cross it and walk ahead to rejoin your car.

Peewits (lapwings) displaying

Preston - Shelley Road Mills and gardens sloping down to the cut

25: Circular walk from Preston

Distance:	8 miles
Time:	4 hours
Parking:	Waterloo Road, Preston
Terrain:	Easy walking all the way. Field paths muddy after rain
Map:	Pathfinder SD 43/53 Preston (North) and Kirkham (Lancs)

This series of walks has now brought you to the southern
terminus of the canal at Preston. Originally the canal started
behind Corporation Street, but now buildings have covered the cut.
Park in Waterloo Road close to the viaduct at Maudlands on the road
route from Preston to Penwortham. Pass under the viaduct and walk
towards the town centre. Continue past the Fylde Tavern and the
Renault garage. Take the reinforced path into a small ornamental
garden and climb the steps to the present-day canal terminus.

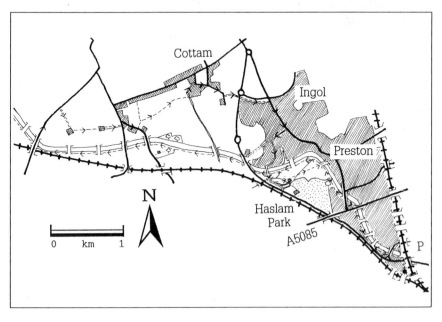

Look for the signpost - hidden by lush September vegetation - which tells you that you are ¹/₂ a mile from the town centre, 7 miles from Catforth and 57 miles from Kendal. Walk on where mallards swim and boys and men fish for bream, roach, perch and pike. Houses on the right have pleasing gardens that slope down to the water's edge. Cross the white-railed bridge, 10, over the Ashton Basin. (Bridges 1 to 8 are on the Glasson Branch of the canal, see Walk 14.) To the right stands Shelley Road Mills, its chimney reflected in the still water.

Pass under bridge 11, the first actually to cross the waterway. The cross beams, and arches with ledges, are much enjoyed by innumerable pigeons. Continue under the modern bridge that carries the road to Blackpool and on past a mill with Tulketh written on it. White water lilies and the pretty amphibious bistort flower on the far side of the tranquil water. Along the wayside flowers common mallow.

Stride on below bridge 12, beyond which is the Lancaster Canal boat club building. To the left is an entrance to Haslam Park. Pass another signpost and then cross an aqueduct, bridge 13, which carries the canal over the fast-flowing Savick Brook. The brook is lined with Indian balsam. Continue below Hollinghead Fold Bridge, 14, a typical Rennie bridge with a curved parapet.

Bulrushes thrust their flower heads to the sky as you approach Ingol Ashes Bridge, 15, which has pointed parapets supporting white railings. Cottam Mill Bridge, 16, also has pointed parapets but no railings. Continue along the much wider towpath, still with houses on both sides, to pass first a winding hole where boats were turned round, and then a modern bridge, 16A, which carries the B6241.

Follow the towpath into the country where the hedgerows of elder, hawthorn and rose carry a profusion of berries. Walk on to bridge 17, a skew bridge. Stroll on to walk below a double row of pylons. Head on to pass below a wooden bridge, of tractor width, sitting on stone abutments. Pass a milestone and carry on to leave the towpath just before bridge 22. Walk left

Mallards

up the slope, then turn right to walk over the bridge and continue along the road. Pass two bungalows and turn right at the access track to Bryars Farm, signposted public footpath.

The track passes below oaks. Pass through a metal gate on the left to walk to the left of a ditch and a hedge. Continue ahead to a stile and then on to take a gate

Elderberries

to the left of a pylon. Walk towards Earl's Farm, passing below the double power lines. The next gate leads into the farmyard and two tall wooden gates give access to another yard. Pass in front of the farmhouse and walk on along the lane to a signposted gate to the road.

Turn left to walk Sidgreaves Lane, passing the women's institute and Lea primary school. At the T-junction, turn right to stride Lea Road. Just before the road bends right, opposite a gracious lodge, look for a public footpath sign on the left side of the road. Walk the faint path, keeping to the left of a ditch, to a footbridge in the right corner of the pasture. Walk on keeping to the left of the hedge to another stile to a footbridge, half-way along. Continue, now with the glorious autumnal hedge to your left, to a field gate in the left corner. Walk ahead to pass through a gap in a wire fence to the left of a pond. Pass through another gap and cross right to a stile in the right corner.

Walk past the pigeon huts, turn right through a farm gate, and then left to walk the farm track to a narrow road. Turn right to walk past houses on the right. Continue along the tree-lined way when it ceases to be metalled. Just beyond a right bend, turn left to stride another attractive, unmade track, Cottam Hall Lane. Pass beneath a road bridge and continue along the track to turn right onto the main road. Walk past the parish church of St Margaret's Ingol, and continue to Hillcrest Avenue, where you turn right.

At Beckshill Road, turn left. Turn left again between the houses, numbers 71 and 73, to rejoin the canal at the delightful Ingol Ashes Bridge, 15. Cross and walk ahead through Haslam Park. Turn left to walk beside the ornamental stream, with its small lake and waterfalls. Look left for a good view of the aqueduct, bridge 13. Continue and rejoin the canal. Turn right to walk to the canal terminus. From here retrace your outward route to rejoin your car.

Hart's tongue fern

Printed by
St Edmundsbury Press, Bury St Edmunds, Suffolk, U.K.